ALSO BY TOM LACALAMITA

THE ULTIMATE BREAD MACHINE COOKBOOK

TOM LACALAMITA

PHOTOGRAPHS BY SIMON METZ

ILLUSTRATIONS BY LAURIE DAVIS

THE ULTIMATE PASTA MACHINE COOKBOOK

SIMON & SCHUSTER

New York London Toronto Sydney Tokyo Singapore

Simon & Schuster
Rockefeller Center
1230 Avenue of the Americas
New York, New York 10020

Designed by Eve Metz
Photographs © 1994 by Simon Metz
Step-by-step illustrations © 1994 by Laurie Davis
Manufactured in the United States of America

3   5   7   9   10   8   6   4   2

Library of Congress Cataloging-in-Publication Data
Lacalamita, Tom.
The ultimate pasta machine cookbook / Tom Lacalamita ;
photographs by Simon Metz,
illustrations by Laurie Davis.
p.   cm.
Includes index.
1. Cookery (Pasta).   2. Pasta products.   I. Title.
TX809.M17L343   1994
641.8'22—DC20   94-30289
                                                          CIP

ISBN: 0-671-50102-X

FOR YAYI AND CRISTINA

ACKNOWLEDGMENTS

To Linda Cunningham, for the opportunity to do this book. To my editor, Patty Leasure, and her assistant, Meaghan Dowling, for their friendship, guidance, and never-ending support. And to the rest of the Simon & Schuster team—Frank Metz, Jackie Seow, Eve Metz, Toni Rachiele, and Joanne Barracca—for their respective contributions along the path of this book's creation.

To Simon Metz and A.J. Battifarano, for their beautiful portrayal of the pastas on film. And Laurie Davis, for the skillful illustrations.

To all of the pasta machine manufacturers, for the use of their appliances.

Sincere thanks to my special friend Glenna Vance, for the nutritional analysis, enthusiasm, and support.

And most important, to my family and friends, for sharing with me my love of food and for the knowledge and skills they have provided and shared with me.

CONTENTS

PART TWO   RECIPES FOR USING FRESH PASTAS AND NOODLES

FOREWORD

As we rapidly approach the year 2000, we are beginning to see the introduction of more and more automatic appliances. Besides being just another kitchen gadget, each of these modern wonders also assists us in developing our culinary abilities to prepare foods that we may have never considered making before.

The first of these marvels was the bread machine, which was introduced in the late 1980s. Even though it was the first automatic appliance capable of preparing food with the push of a button, it was received with total skepticism. But that was then and this is now. With well over 4 million households owning bread machines today, people have begun to look toward other appliances to perform the same feat: automatically prepared food with the simple push of a button. Now, with the introduction of the pasta machine, it appears that we may not have to look much further.

Automatic pasta machines are an invaluable kitchen appliance if understood and used properly. As we have become more and more concerned with increasing our dietary intake of complex carbohydrates, pasta consumption has continued to grow—and what better way to enjoy pasta and noodles than by making them at home, automatically with a pasta machine?

As the marketing and product manager for a leading appliance manufacturer, I have had the opportunity to work with a wide variety of automatic appliances. Combining this experience with my food and cooking background, I am very pleased to present to you my interpretations of authentic Mediterranean and Asian pastas, noodles, and dumplings, all of which are easily made with an automatic pasta machine. And to entice and encourage you to use your pasta machine as often as possible, I have also developed a series of appetizing recipes for sauces, soups, entrées, and desserts to prepare with your homemade pasta.

This collection of recipes has been triple-tested in nine of the most popular pasta machines. I have made many pounds of pasta, noodles, and dumplings in developing and fine-tuning these recipes so that they work equally well in all models without the need for adaptations.

When using this cookbook, be sure to measure carefully, use the very best ingredients available, and above all, get to know your pasta machine by reading all the materials provided by your manufacturer. I am certain that once you get the hang of it, you will wonder how you ever lived on store-bought pasta and prepared sauces.

INTRODUCTION

WHY AN AUTOMATIC PASTA MACHINE?

My INITIAL REACTION when I first saw an automatic pasta machine was quite similar to what I felt the first time I was introduced to "R2D2," my automatic bread machine—total skepticism. Having been brought up eating wonderful dried durum-wheat pasta from Italy, dumplings, and other egg pastas purchased from local pasta or Asian food stores, and, when the urge struck, homemade noodles, I was at a loss to see the need for another "do-it-yourself" appliance. But, then again, I gave the bread machine a chance seven years ago with great results, so the least I could do was make a pound of pasta.

Although the instructions were somewhat vague and the recipes limited, I carefully read them, measured the ingredients, and tied on my apron. So far so good. I put the dried ingredients in the pasta-machine mixing bowl, flipped the switch, and slowly added the beaten eggs and oil. Even as the ingredients began to come together in coarse lumps, I wasn't yet totally convinced. Having made pounds of egg pasta with my faithful, hand-cranked Atlas pasta machine, I was still suspicious of this newfangled appliance.

When the time came to extrude the dough I braced myself for the unknown. Would the dough come out as anticipated or would I wind up with a solid mass of flour and eggs? After a few seconds of grunting and groaning, fine, thin strands of fettuccine began to gradually appear through the extruder die. At first somewhat gnarled and twisted, the fettuccine began to extrude perfectly formed and silken, the same as when made by hand. The only difference was that rather than my having to mix and knead the ingredients and then crank them out by hand, the pasta machine was doing it all automatically and in almost no time at all.

After a few more attempts, using more exotic ingredients, such as buckwheat flour and vegetable purées, I began to look at the pasta machine in a new light. Before I knew it I was making mental lists of all the pastas and noodles I wanted to try, especially those that were not readily available at my local stores and that were too time-consuming to make by hand, the old-fashioned way. I was once again hooked. This new kitchen helper was doing the hard work and I was taking all the credit. The only thing I had to worry about was using the proper ingredients and measuring them accurately.

PASTA AND NOODLES: WEST MEETS EAST

WE WILL MOST LIKELY never know where the concept of making a paste of ground grains and liquid and cooking it in hot water originated. We do know, however, that grains were being cultivated for consumption over ten thousand years ago. Perhaps some prehistoric individual accidentally dropped a piece of unleavened bread dough or a spoonful of cereal mush in a cooking vessel of hot water and liked the texture and taste. Nevertheless, whoever the first individual was, he or she should be credited with creating an industry that in the United States alone sold close to $1.9 billion of dried pasta in 1989. It is also estimated that close to 4.8 billion pounds of dried and fresh pasta were consumed in the United States in 1991. As dramatic as the numbers may seem, they are almost meaningless when you take into consideration that while the average pasta consumption per person in the United States in 1991 was nineteen pounds, in Italy it was estimated to be fifty-five pounds. And if we were able to quantify pasta consumption in China, the numbers would become even more overwhelming.

We do know, however, that by 3000 B.C., the Chinese were consuming noodles made from wheat, corn, rice, and other starches. Therefore, it wasn't Marco Polo after all who introduced pasta to Asia. In fact, Marco probably picked up a tip or two on noodle making from the Chinese and brought it back with him to Venice. While the Chinese were making thin- and wide-cut noodles and wrapping pieces of dough around savory fillings, this concept of pasta was relatively unknown in the West. The pasta consumed in the Italian peninsula, and for that matter, most of Europe, consisted of freshly made gnocchilike dumplings and sheets of lasagnelike pasta that were usually boiled, fried, or baked. In fact, there are even references in Roman writings that refer to *laganum*, the forerunner of today's lasagne. Thinner-cut pastas, like spaghetti, and the more familiar tubular shapes, like ziti, would not be known until the Saracen Arabic domination of Sicily in A.D. 831.

As world travelers, the Arabs collected and assimilated many different cultures and customs. In turn, they left lasting traces of their influence in the areas they conquered. Having learned pasta making from the Persians, the Saracens taught the same methods to the inhabitants of Sicily. Primarily occupying hot, arid locations, the Saracens developed ways of making pasta without using perishable ingredients, so they could dry the pasta in the sun. In order to do so, the dough had to be rolled and cut very thin so that it could dry quickly. The first example of this type of pasta in Europe is found in Sicily, where dough made from hard wheat and water was rolled around long, thin pieces of reed, which were then removed, leaving behind a tube of spaghettilike pasta with a hollow center. The pasta was then put out under the hot sun to dry, extending its shelf life by months. Curiously enough, this forerunner of macaroni is still made at home in Sicily today.

The first commercial production of macaroni (dried pasta made with hard wheat and water) took place in Arab Sicily and continued throughout Italy, where it was prepared with whatever ingredients were available in various sizes, shapes, and methods.

Pasta became very fashionable during the Renaissance, when extravagant dishes and preparations were created. Interestingly, simple hard-wheat macaroni became the sustenance of the poor, and stalls selling macaroni with grated cheese sprang up in cities and large towns throughout southern Italy. It was not until the 1800s, however, that a suitable commercial application was developed to effectively mass-produce macaroni that could be dried and stored for extended periods of time without spoiling. Today over 90 percent of all pasta products are made from processes based on this preservation method. The pasta is made from golden durum-wheat flour and water, and the ingredients are mixed and then extruded through brass dies. The extruded macaroni is then dried in such a way that it dries evenly and is not brittle. In effect, the process used in automatic pasta machines is not unlike that used by the commercial producers. The only difference is that the pasta and macaroni you are making will be eaten right away or frozen for later use.

PASTA: THE KEY TO A MORE HEALTHFUL DIET

THE INCREASE of pasta consumption in the United States from 11.5 pounds per person in 1975 to 19 pounds in 1991 is by no means accidental. In 1990, the U.S. government redefined the four basic food groups and introduced a newly designed Food Pyramid. Complex carbohydrates, which include the grains and cereals, are now the foundation of the pyramid. After years of being told that complex carbohydrates were high in calories, we are now advised that in order to lower the incidence of chronic disease and diabetes, we should increase our consumption of complex carbohydrates by 50 percent and substantially reduce the amount of animal protein, fats, and sugar in our diet. The only problem is, how do we increase our intake of carbohydrates and, at the same time, maintain an appetizing diet? Interestingly enough, the Italians and Chinese have been doing this for hundreds of years. At least 65 percent of the calories consumed in China come from complex carbohydrates in the form of grains and cereals and, since we know that the Chinese place a major emphasis on the consumption of noodles, a good portion of these calories can be attributed to them.

Durum-wheat pasta (page 33), for example, simply made from wheat flour and water,

FOOD GUIDE PYRAMID
A GUIDE TO DAILY FOOD CHOICES

KEY   F = Fat (naturally   S = Sugars
occurring   (added)
and added)

Fats, Oils, & Sweets
USE SPARINGLY

These symbols show that fat and added sugars come mostly from fats, oils, and sweets, but can be part of or added to foods from the other food groups as well.

Milk, Yogurt, & Cheese Group
2-3 SERVINGS

Meat, Poultry, Fish, Dry Beans, Eggs, & Nuts Group
2-3 SERVINGS

Vegetable Group
3-5 SERVINGS

Fruit Group
2-4 SERVINGS

Bread, Cereal, Rice, & Pasta Group
6-11 SERVINGS

SOURCE: U.S. Department of Agriculture / U.S. Department of Health and Human Services

Use the Food Guide Pyramid to help you eat better every day...the Dietary Guidelines way. Start with plenty of Breads, Cereals, Rice, and Pasta; Vegetables; and Fruits. Add two to three servings from the Milk group and two to three servings from the Meat group. Each of these food groups provides some, but not all, of the nutrients you need. No one food group is more important than the other—for good health you need them all. Go easy on fats, oils, and sweets, the foods in the small tip of the Pyramid.

is naturally high in complex carbohydrates and low in fat, calories, sodium, and cholesterol. Durum-wheat pasta also contains six of the eight essential amino acids necessary for a healthy diet. When pasta is served with small portions of meat, poultry, seafood, vegetables, or dairy products, a well-balanced, complete meal can easily be made.

This brings us to another point. In Italy, pasta is eaten almost daily and is a part of the national culinary heritage, while in Asia, noodles are considered to be a convenience food. This outlook has become prevalent in the United States. Recently, a study on eating trends showed that aside from consuming pasta for health reasons, people see pasta as a convenience food with a universal appeal to all age groups.

By using your automatic pasta machine wisely, you will be able to effortlessly prepare an endless variety of delicious, wholesome pastas and noodles. By adding other ingredients, such as puréed vegetables or whole-grain flours, you will also be able to increase the nutritional value, cup for cup, of the pastas you are making.

Now that you can easily make fresh pasta at home, perhaps you will consider making it a part of your daily diet. In order for you to do so, I have prepared and included recipes for favorite sauces, soups, entrées, and desserts that include pasta or noodles. For the most part, they are easy to prepare and are low in fat and cholesterol. Each pasta or noodle recipe also includes recommended sauces or serving suggestions. To make it easier for you to assess your dietary intake, all of the recipes come with a complete nutritional analysis.

MAKING PASTA AUTOMATICALLY

AUTOMATIC PASTA MACHINES are extremely versatile. Made up of motor and housing, a mixing bowl, an extruder, and extruder dies, the machine mixes the ingredients to develop the gluten, a natural protein found in wheat and other grains that gives pasta its elasticity when extruded, or rolled out. Once the dough has been mixed and kneaded, it is then forced out through the narrow openings of the extruder dies. The extruded pasta is cut at the desired lengths and is then put aside for approximately thirty minutes to let the gluten relax before being cooked. Couldn't be simpler, right? Well, if you have ever gone through this process you will know that the best intentions don't always give you the best results. There are many variables that affect how the pasta comes out, and understanding how to control these variables will enable you to make perfect pasta every time.

Having made pasta by hand for years and having used all of the different brands and models of automatic pasta machines, I have come to understand how the different machines work. I have also learned how to get the pasta and noodles to look and taste as expected, and I hope that you will find this information, along with the recipes, and the troubleshooting guide in the last chapter, extremely useful.

First and foremost, take the time to read carefully the manufacturer's owner's manual. It is imperative that you completely understand how your pasta machine is designed to work. If you have ever made pasta by hand, you will know that there is no such thing as an exact recipe. For example, a recipe may call for "3 large eggs and 2½ to 3 cups of flour, depending on the consistency of the dough." For the novice cook, this may be a bit daunting. The reason for this inexactitude is that flour, which can constitute up to 60 percent of the weight of the pasta, contains varying amounts of moisture. Part of the moisture is inherent in the wheat at the time it is harvested and then ground into flour. Ambient humidity also can increase the moisture content of the flour.

Even though the pasta and noodle recipes I developed for this cookbook were carefully triple-tested in the most popular models, there are many variables that can determine success or failure. Ideally, the normal ratio of dry to liquid ingredients is 4 parts flour to 1 part liquid. While this may appear to be very simple, do not be deceived.

When making pasta by hand, you can fine-tune the recipe by touching the dough to see whether or not it is too sticky and requires additional flour to make it all come together in a smooth, soft ball. With a pasta machine, even if you followed the recipe to the letter and measured carefully, if the dough is not the right consistency, it may not extrude properly. It usually only takes about three minutes of mixing for the dough to be properly kneaded. The dough should appear to be coming together in soft, pea-sized crumbs. Dough that is too dry will appear crumbly and look like piecrust or biscuit dough before liquid is added to it. The pasta dough may crumble when extruded, or it will have white streaks running through it. If this is the case, stop extruding. Open the mixing-bowl lid and remove a very small amount of dough. Squeeze the dough between your thumb and index finger. If the dough has white spots in it, it is definitely too dry and needs additional liquid. Close the lid and start mixing the dough again. Add additional water through the feed tube, a teaspoon at a time, until the dough appears to have a smoother consistency. Remember, do not add too much water or the dough will be too soft and the pasta machine will have difficulty extruding efficiently. Let the dough knead for sixty seconds and then resume extruding.

In the event that the extruder die appears to be buckling or bending while the pasta begins to extrude, stop extruding immediately before you damage either the die or the appliance. The dough is either not well kneaded or is too dry. Look at the dough. If it is not the proper consistency, let it continue kneading a minute or two longer. If the dough appears to be too dry, add additional water as explained above.

If the dough is too soft and the pasta is sticking together, or in the case of tubular pastas like ziti, collapsing, you may have to add additional flour. My recommendation is to do this only if you feel that the pasta is very bad. In all of my attempts to add more flour, the results have varied from fair to mediocre. Since the dough has already been kneaded and the gluten developed, the additional flour may not be incorporated properly, and you might be better off starting over again using less water. To try and remedy the problem, stop kneading, open the lid, and add a tablespoon or two of additional flour. Let the dough knead for one to two minutes longer before extruding again.

It is imperative that the extruder die be soaked in a small bowl of hot tap water (100° to 110° F) 30 seconds before placing it on the extruder. This will enable the first strands of pasta to come out smoothly.

When the pasta is ready to extrude, be prepared to help it along. When extruding thin strands like angel hair, spaghetti, linguine, and fettuccine, gently run your fingers through the pasta as it is being extruded so that the strands do not stick together. The best way to cut this kind of pasta is either with a pair of kitchen scissors or with a paring knife. If using a knife, cut from the bottom up for best results, since the strand ends will not stick together.

When tubular-shaped pasta such as ziti is extruded, it sometimes curls. If you can, bend the pasta to make it straight, but be careful not to break it. Cut this type of pasta with a paring knife in a downward motion so that the pasta falls gently on your hand or work surface. Do not cut tubular pastas with a scissor, since the ends will mesh together.

Sometimes the extruding pasta may appear to be stuck. If enough dough to hold on to has already been extruded, you can gently pull on it to help things along.

Usually, toward the end, the dough may have kneaded into pieces or balls that are too large to fit through the extruder. If this appears to be the case, or if the dough stays toward the back of the mixing bowl, stop the appliance. Open the lid and tear the dough into small, marble-sized pieces and drop them toward the front of the mixing bowl near the extruder opening. You may have to do this a couple of times if you want to extrude all the dough.

You would be surprised how dried dough, left in a pasta machine, resembles cement. Never, I repeat, never leave leftover or unextruded dough in a pasta maker for an extended period of time. In fact, try to make pasta only when you know that you will not be interrupted. As the pasta dough sits, it begins to dry out, which will seriously affect whether or not the dough will extrude properly or at all.

CLEANUP AND CARE

CLEANING AN AUTOMATIC PASTA MACHINE may appear to be a challenge, because of the numerous parts involved. In addition, stuck-on residual dough can be difficult to remove. In testing the recipes, I discovered a couple of cleanup tips that may provide some assistance.

Always disassemble the pasta machine after making your last batch of pasta for the day. If the extruder and housing appear to be very sticky or have dough stuck to them that is difficult to remove, let them air-dry for a few hours or overnight. Once the dough is completely dry, it will flake off easily.

Always wash the extruder, the dies, the mixing bowl, and the lid with cool, never hot, water. Hot water will cook the dough in place and make it more difficult to remove. To remove stuck pieces of dough from the dies, soak them overnight in a small container of cool water. Unclog any openings with a hat pin or a nut pick.

Unplug the housing before cleaning and wipe down with a clean, damp cloth or sponge. If necessary, use mild dishwashing liquid (never any harsh chemical detergents) when washing the components. Towel-dry when done.

HELP IS BUT A PHONE CALL AWAY

FOR BEST RESULTS in making pasta automatically with the flip of a switch, just remember these few suggestions:

- Get to know your pasta machine by reading the owner's manual.
- Be willing to experiment until you get the right ratio of flour to liquid. Do not become frustrated if your first attempts do not turn out 100 percent as expected. The odds are that although the pasta may not be picture-perfect, it probably tastes fine.
- Also, do not forget that the best source for information on how to use your automatic pasta machine is the manufacturer. All the manufacturers have fully staffed customer-service departments with trained representatives who are more than happy to answer your questions.

TAKING IT TO THE NEXT STEP

WHILE MUCH EMPHASIS is put on making pasta automatically with the flip of a switch, many people overlook what I believe to be the greatest joy and asset of the pasta machine

—being able to use the extruded dough to make hand-shaped pastas like tortellini, ravioli, and cavatelli, and even Chinese won tons, pot stickers, and beggar's purses, to mention only a few possibilities.

All automatic pasta machines have a lasagne die, which extrudes approximately two-inch-wide flat pieces of dough. This dough is the basis for making an endless variety of hand-shaped pasta creations.

Since the lasagne noodles extruded from the pasta machine are, in my opinion, too thick to use as is, they can easily be made thinner and wider by rolling the dough out with a rolling pin, or if you are fortunate enough to have one, through a hand-cranked pasta maker. Now you may be asking yourself, "Isn't this defeating the purpose of ease and simplicity if I have to hand-roll the dough?" The answer is no. What you are now able to do is expand your pasta repertoire to make pastas and dumplings that you may have enjoyed at restaurants or overseas and can now make at home. Just bear in mind that the pasta machine is still going to do the hard work of making and extruding the dough. You have the creative job of hand-shaping and filling the pasta or dumplings. And once you have made your own ravioli or won tons by following the simple yet delicious recipes that follow, anything else you may purchase in the supermarket frozen food case will be tasteless in comparison.

When making hand-shaped pastas or dumplings, allow yourself sufficient time to prepare the dough and fillings and then for the hand-shaping. The time spent will be definitely worth the effort!

Bear in mind that you will wind up with small scraps after cutting the dough pieces as specified in the hand-shaped pasta recipes. Do not try to recycle this dough by putting it back in the pasta machine to be extruded again. It will not work. Either discard or save by freezing in tightly sealed plastic bags. When you have accumulated approximately a pound, you can try making Noodle Pudding (page 173). You can also cut the scraps into small strips to be served with Chicken Soup (page 136) as if they were Maltagliati (page 80), which are free-form Italian noodles.

COOKING AND STORING PASTA AND NOODLES

You SHOULD ALWAYS let homemade pasta and noodles rest for 30 minutes before cooking. One pound of pasta or noodles should be cooked in 4 quarts of water. Fill a large saucepan with water and bring to a boil (never add oil to the cooking water, since it will make the pasta or noodles slippery and the sauce will not stick well to it). Add 1½ to 2 teaspoons of salt once the water boils. When the water begins its second boil, add the pasta. The exact cooking time of pasta varies according to the shape, size, and type of pasta or noodle being cooked. Altitude and temperature of the pasta (whether it is at room temperature, refrigerated, or frozen) will also determine how long it will take for the water to resume boiling after the pasta has been added. The following chart can be used as a point of reference. The cooking times are from the time the water starts to boil after the pasta has been added:

Homemade pasta	Cooking times	Homemade pasta	Cooking times
Angel hair	1 to 2 minutes	Broad noodles, such as	
Spaghetti	2 to 3 minutes	lasagne, manicotti,	
Fettuccine	2 to 4 minutes	pappardelle, and farfalle	2 to 3 minutes
Ziti and penne	2 to 4 minutes	Ravioli and tortelloni	4 to 6 minutes
Orecchiette and		Tortellini and cappelletti	3 to 5 minutes
cavatelli	4 to 5 minutes	Agnolotti	3 to 5 minutes
Gnocchi	2 to 3 minutes	All Asian noodles	2 to 3 minutes

Cook pasta or noodles, stirring gently, periodically. Test for doneness about three-quarters of the way through the cooking time. Pasta should be tender but firm. Drain immediately. Unless otherwise specified in the recipe, always reserve a small amount of water after the pasta has drained so that the noodles are not totally dry. Place the pasta in a large serving bowl and prepare with sauce, or if you are preparing a salad or Asian noodle dish, follow that recipe for the next step.

Most uncooked pastas and noodles, with the exception of gnocchi, can be stored for later use. Extruded strands of pasta—such as angel hair, spaghetti, and Asian noodles—should be lightly sprinkled with flour and gently tossed with your fingers so that they do not stick together. Spread them on a clean kitchen cloth and let sit for 30 minutes. Spread tubular-shaped pasta like penne and ziti, and hand-cut pastas and noodles, in a single layer on a clean kitchen cloth and let it sit for 30 minutes.

These pastas and noodles can be stored uncooked in the refrigerator for up to two days. Place on a large tray or serving platter covered with a cloth. Spread pasta or noodles in a single layer and cover with another cloth. They can also be frozen in tightly sealed plastic bags for up to three months. Be sure to squeeze out all the air.

Pasta shells for manicotti, cannelloni, and lasagne should be cooked before they are stored in the refrigerator or freezer; otherwise they would dry out and become brittle or warp. Once they are cooked, rinse under cold water and drain on a clean kitchen cloth. When dry, stack with pieces of waxed paper or parchment between the pasta. Store in tightly sealed plastic bags, with the air squeezed out, for up to two days in the refrigerator and three months in the freezer.

Hand-shaped pastas and dumplings like tortellini, ravioli, and won tons are best cooked the same day or stored in the freezer in flat, plastic containers. Do not layer more than two high, and place a piece of waxed paper or parchment in between the layers. Use within one month.

Frozen pasta and noodles should not be defrosted before cooking. Place straight from the freezer in boiling water. Allow additional time for cooking, which will vary depending on the type and shape of the pasta or noodle.

INGREDIENTS

ALL AUTOMATIC PASTA MACHINES basically perform the same way, although mechanically there are differences. Some models have more powerful motors and a larger capacity and therefore can handle large amounts of ingredients to make up to three pounds of pasta or noodles. Since we are accustomed to purchasing pasta in one-pound quantities, all of the recipes I have developed are for this amount and will perform equally well in all brands and models of machines.

Since the flour and salt are always placed in the pasta-machine mixing bowl first, and the liquids, including eggs and vegetable purées, are poured in afterward and separately through the feed tube, I have divided the pasta ingredients into two groups: Dry Ingredients and Liquid Ingredients. Only pour the liquid ingredients through the feed tube once the pasta machine is turned on; otherwise they may not mix evenly with the dry ingredients.

FLOUR

Wheat is the only grain that has a high enough protein content (gluten) to make it ideal for making extruded pastas and noodles. As the dough is mixed and kneaded, the gluten comes in contact with the liquid ingredients, forming an interlocking network of elastic strands. This is what gives pasta its ''bite.''

When different types of wheat are milled, they produce different kinds of flour with varying levels of gluten. When making pasta with eggs, a low-level gluten flour, such as unbleached, all-purpose, gives the best results. For the most part, this pasta is softer, with less of a bite, than durum-wheat pasta. The eggs also act as a binder to keep the dough together and provide some elasticity.

On the other hand, macaroni—pasta made from only flour and water—is best made with golden durum-wheat flour (also referred to by some as pasta flour). This flour has a very high gluten content and produces a firmer dough and, subsequently, pasta with more of a bite. I do not recommend using unbleached, all-purpose flour when making this type of pasta. The quality and taste are not worth the trouble. Furthermore, since durum-wheat flour is the same type of flour used by the commercial producers of dried macaroni, the pasta you will be making will be just as good, if not better. Although I usually do not like recommending ingredients that are not readily available in local supermarkets, flours from golden durum wheat are a worthwhile exception. Some specialty-food stores sell durum wheat and semolina flour, which is coarsely ground golden durum wheat. They can also be ordered through some mail-order catalogues (see Source Directory).

When using whole-wheat flour to make pasta, try to purchase stone-ground flour from a reliable source, such as a mail-order catalogue. The quality of the flour will probably be better than what is sold in the supermarket, and the pasta will definitely taste better.

Some pastas and noodles are made with buckwheat and rice flours. Both of these flours have no gluten whatsoever, and therefore, in order to get them to work well in a pasta machine, they must be mixed with a high-gluten flour. Bread flour, which is sold in most supermarkets, is ideal to use. Milled from hard winter wheat, it is higher in gluten than unbleached, all-purpose flour, yet it is not as high as durum wheat, which is too strong for these types of pastas and noodles. Bread flour is also used for making Chinese noodles, since it is similar to the type of flour used in Asia.

When I make pasta by hand, I always sift the flour after I have measured it. Sifting makes flour lighter and easier for liquid ingredients to blend with it. In testing the different pasta recipes, I tried both unsifted and sifted flour. I most definitely recommend the sifted version. The dough appears smoother and the pasta extrudes with ease almost every time.

To measure flour accurately, never dip the measuring cup into the bag of flour, since air pockets can occur and you may not get a full cup of flour. Spoon the flour, a tablespoon at a time, into the measuring cup. Stick a blunt-ended knife into the flour a couple of times to break up any air pockets or clumps. Level off with the straight edge of the knife.

LIQUIDS

The liquid ingredients bind the dry ingredients together. The most commonly used liquids in making pasta are water, eggs, oil, and vegetable purées. All liquid ingredients should be at room temperature unless specified otherwise.

Always use large eggs, which are approximately ¼ cup of liquid. Nevertheless, this is not always the case. In order to have the correct ratio of liquid to dry ingredients always measure the liquid ingredients in an 8-ounce Pyrex glass measuring cup. Break the eggs directly into the cup. Add whatever other liquid ingredients are called for in the recipe, including vegetable purées. If the total volume of liquids does not equal ¾ of a cup, add more liquid as specified in the recipe. If called for in the recipe, lightly beat the liquid ingredients together in the Pyrex measuring cup only after you have confirmed that they equal ¾ of a cup, since beaten eggs may increase in volume, giving the impression that you have more than ¾ cup of liquid.

When vegetables are called for in a pasta recipe, they should be puréed as fine as baby food. In fact, a simple way to make flavored pastas like carrot or beet is to use a 4-ounce jar of strained baby food.

Tools of the Trade

Since you have already invested in an automatic pasta machine, you might as well go the extra mile and spend a few dollars more to equip yourself with the necessary accessories to make your pasta and noodles even more professional-looking. Most of these accessories are available in any good housewares store.

MEASURING CUPS AND SPOONS

Even though some pasta machines come with their own measuring cups, I have found that although they can be useful, they are not entirely necessary. You can use any U.S. standard measuring cups as long as you do not exceed three cups of flour when making pasta in those models. If you do not own U.S. standard measuring cups, purchase easy-to-read plastic or metal ones for dry measuring in ¼-, ⅓-, ½-, ⅔-, ¾-, and 1-cup capacities. Also purchase an 8-ounce glass Pyrex measuring cup for measuring liquids, and metal or plastic measuring spoons in ¼-, ½-, and 1-teaspoon capacities, and ½- and 1-tablespoon.

SIFTER

A sifter is a mesh-bottomed kitchen utensil, available in metal and plastic. Dry ingredients are passed through the bottom in order to make them lighter and to remove any large particles.

KITCHEN TIMER

Next to measuring properly, timing is a key element to successful pasta. A rotary kitchen timer that rings at the designated moment will let you know exactly when the pasta machine has kneaded for three minutes.

PARING KNIFE

A paring knife is short-bladed and traditionally used to peel fruits and vegetables. I find the size of this knife to be the most practical to cut the pasta as it is extruded from the machine.

PASTRY WHEEL

A pastry wheel is a utensil with a sharp metal disk attached to a short wooden handle. The wheel rotates, enabling it to be used as a cutting tool. There are two basic types of pastry wheels: those with a plain cutting edge and those with a fluted edge. Some have two wheels, one of each type. This is the most practical.

FOOD MILL

A food mill is a valuable kitchen helper in puréeing different foods. It is also important when straining tomatoes for sauces or preparing potatoes for gnocchi. In a manner resembling that of a mechanical sieve, food is forced through a strainer plate that removes skin, seeds, and fibers. Most food mills come with interchangeable plates with small holes for finely strained foods and larger holes for coarser results.

HAND-CRANKED PASTA MAKER

A chrome-plated or stainless-steel manually operated machine, consisting of a pair of smooth rollers for rolling out sheets of pasta dough, and a double pair of notched rollers for rolling out and cutting dough for noodles.

PART ONE

FRESH PASTA
AUTOMATICALLY

HIGH COMPLEX-CARBOHYDRATE PASTAS

BASIC EGG AND FLAVORED PASTAS

HAND-CUT AND STUFFED PASTAS

ASIAN NOODLES

HIGH COMPLEX-CARBOHYDRATE PASTAS

PASTAS HIGH IN COMPLEX CARBOHYDRATES are easy to make in your automatic pasta machine. Made either with durum-wheat flour or unbleached, all-purpose flour and other grains, these pastas have been made and enjoyed for hundreds of years.

The pastas in this chapter are rich in B vitamins, fiber, and iron. They are also extremely high in complex carbohydrates, which supply the body with energy in a constant time-released manner. For this reason, athletes consume 60 to 70 percent of their calories in complex carbohydrates before athletic events in order to have a supply of sustained energy.

When these pastas are served with sauces made from meats, vegetables, and dairy products, the nutritional value is increased, not to mention the delicious variety of pasta dishes.

DURUM-WHEAT PASTA
(PASTASCIUTTA)

Historians are unable to pinpoint the exact period when *pastasciutta*, or macaroni and spaghetti as we know it, was first eaten on the Italian peninsula. With zero cholesterol and no added fat, this is the simplest homemade pasta to make.

Available dry in hundreds of shapes, sizes, and thicknesses, pastasciutta is made from the golden kernel of durum wheat. High in gluten, finely ground durum-wheat pasta flour is available at some specialty shops and from mail-order catalogues (page 184).

Use this recipe to make an endless variety of pasta shapes, such as spaghetti, linguine, and ziti.

DRY INGREDIENTS
3 cups durum-wheat flour (finely ground
    pasta flour), sifted

LIQUID INGREDIENTS
¾ cup water

Following the instructions given in your owner's manual, prepare and set up the pasta machine with an extruder die to make the desired shape of pasta.

All ingredients must be at room temperature. Add the dry ingredients to the pasta machine mixing bowl. Switch the pasta machine on. Slowly pour the liquid ingredients through the feed tube. Mix for approximately 3 minutes, or until the dough appears to be coming together in soft, pea-sized crumbs.

Following the instructions given in your owner's manual, begin to extrude the dough. Cut off the first 2 to 3 inches extruded and discard. As the pasta begins to come out, gently move it away from the machine. Cut with a sharp paring knife or scissors at desired lengths. Place extruded pasta on a wire rack or on a clean kitchen cloth. Let sit for at least 30 minutes before cooking, or store for later use (page 23).

FOUR 4-OUNCE SERVINGS

RECOMMENDED SAUCES AND DISHES: Durum-wheat pasta is probably the most universal of all and can be served with any type of sauce or accompaniment desired.

APPROXIMATE NUTRITIONAL ANALYSIS PER SERVING WITHOUT SAUCE
451 calories, 16g protein, 91g carbohydrates, 86g complex carbohydrates, 1g fat, 0mg cholesterol, 3mg sodium, 233mg potassium

VENETIAN WHOLE-WHEAT PASTA
(BIGOLI)

Bigoli, a specialty of Venice and the Veneto region of Italy, is the only true Italian pasta made with whole-wheat flour. This pasta is ideal to make in a pasta machine, since the dough is typically extruded through a small cylindrical tool called a *bigalaro,* which forms thick strands of spaghettilike pasta.

While normal spaghetti is usually about 12 inches long, bigoli can be as long as 15 inches, making it a slight challenge to twirl when eating!

DRY INGREDIENTS

3 cups whole-wheat flour, sifted
$^1/_2$ teaspoon salt

LIQUID INGREDIENTS

2 large eggs, lightly beaten with
$^1/_4$ cup plus 1 tablespoon lukewarm milk
1 tablespoon sweet butter, melted in the
  milk

Following the instructions given in your owner's manual, prepare and set up the pasta machine with the spaghetti extruder die.

All ingredients must be at room temperature. Place the liquid ingredients in a glass measuring cup. If less than $^3/_4$ cup, add some milk to make up the balance.

Add the dry ingredients to the pasta machine mixing bowl. Switch the pasta machine on. Slowly pour the liquid ingredients through the feed tube. Mix for approximately 3 minutes, or until the dough appears to be coming together in soft, pea-sized crumbs.

Following the instructions given in your owner's manual, begin to extrude the dough. Cut off the first 2 to 3 inches extruded and discard. As the pasta begins to come out, gently move it away from the machine. Cut with a sharp paring knife or scissors at desired lengths. Place extruded pasta on a wire rack or on a clean kitchen cloth. Let the pasta sit for at least 30 minutes before cooking, or store for later use (page 23).

FOUR 4-OUNCE SERVINGS

RECOMMENDED SAUCES: Tomato Sauce (page 96), Wild Mushroom Sauce (page 119), Butter and Sage Sauce (page 122)

APPROXIMATE NUTRITIONAL ANALYSIS PER SERVING WITHOUT SAUCE

387 calories, 17g protein, 67g carbohydrates, 52g complex carbohydrates, 8g fat, 139mg cholesterol, 319mg sodium, 431mg potassium

BUCKWHEAT PASTA
(PIZZOCCHERI)

Buckwheat is enjoyed in many cultures and in many different guises. In the Valtellina area of Lombardy, buckwheat pasta—or *pizzoccheri*, as it is known—is a specialty of the region. This distinctly flavored pasta is especially delicious when combined with a rustic wild mushroom sauce or with browned butter and sage.

Since buckwheat flour has no gluten, you have to mix it with high-gluten wheat flour to help strengthen the dough. Bread flour, available in most supermarkets, is a good choice. Pizzoccheri are best when extruded with the fettuccine die and cut in 4- to 6-inch lengths.

DRY INGREDIENTS

2 cups bread flour, sifted with
1 cup white buckwheat flour
½ teaspoon salt

LIQUID INGREDIENTS

2 large eggs, lightly beaten with
¼ cup milk

Following the instructions given in your owner's manual, prepare and set up the pasta machine with the fettuccine extruder die.

All ingredients must be at room temperature. Place the liquid ingredients in a glass measuring cup. If less than ¾ cup, add more milk to make up the balance.

Add the dry ingredients to the pasta machine mixing bowl. Switch the pasta machine on. Slowly pour the liquid ingredients through the feed tube. Mix for approximately 3 minutes, or until the dough resembles soft, pea-sized crumbs.

Following the instructions given in your owner's manual, begin to extrude the dough. Cut off the first 2 to 3 inches extruded and discard. As the pasta begins to come out, gently move it away from the machine. Cut with a sharp paring knife or scissors at desired lengths. Place extruded pasta on a clean kitchen cloth. Cover with another cloth and let sit for at least 30 minutes before cooking, or store for later use (page 23).

FOUR 4-OUNCE SERVINGS

RECOMMENDED SAUCES: Veal Ragù and Wild Mushroom Sauce (page 108), Salmon and Lemon Sauce (page 113), Wild Mushroom Sauce (page 119), Butter and Sage Sauce (page 122), Pesto Sauce (page 123)

APPROXIMATE NUTRITIONAL ANALYSIS PER SERVING WITHOUT SAUCE

364 calories, 14g protein, 66g carbohydrates, 60g complex carbohydrates, 5g fat, 131mg cholesterol, 316mg sodium, 268mg potassium

CORNMEAL PASTA

(PASTA DI MAIS)

In the more remote areas of northern Italy, corn, which was introduced from the Americas, helped to overcome the problem of providing food in a region that was agriculturally deficient. Even today, polenta and cornmeal pasta are still popular dishes in northern Italy.

Cornmeal pasta combines well with a hearty meat or vegetable sauce. Use high-quality finely ground cornmeal for the best results.

DRY INGREDIENTS

2 cups unbleached, all-purpose flour
  sifted with
1 cup cornmeal
½ teaspoon salt

LIQUID INGREDIENTS

3 large eggs, lightly beaten with
1½ tablespoons extra-virgin olive oil

Following the instructions given in your owner's manual, prepare and set up the pasta machine with an extruder die to make the desired shape of pasta. For best results, extrude using round tubular dies, such as those for making penne or ziti.

All ingredients must be at room temperature. Place the liquid ingredients in a glass measuring cup. If less than ¾ cup, add some water to make up the balance.

Add the dry ingredients to the pasta machine mixing bowl. Switch the pasta machine on. Slowly pour the liquid ingredients through the feed tube. Mix for approximately 2 to 3 minutes, or until the dough appears to be coming together in soft, pea-sized crumbs.

Following the instructions given in your owner's manual, begin to extrude the dough. Cut off the first 2 to 3 inches extruded and discard. As the pasta begins to come out, gently move it away from the machine. Cut with a sharp paring knife or scissors at desired lengths. Place extruded pasta on a wire rack or on a clean kitchen cloth. Let sit for at least 30 minutes before cooking, or store for later use (page 23).

FOUR 4-OUNCE SERVINGS

RECOMMENDED SAUCES: Marinara Sauce (page 99), Puttanesca Sauce (page 100), Veal Ragù and Wild Mushroom Sauce (page 108), Broccoli and Onion Sauce (page 114), Wild Mushroom Sauce (page 119), Zucchini with Garlic and Olive Oil (page 120), Butter and Sage Sauce (page 122)

APPROXIMATE NUTRITIONAL ANALYSIS PER SERVING WITHOUT SAUCE

451 calories, 15g protein, 72g carbohydrates, 65g complex carbohydrates, 11g fat, 193mg cholesterol, 68mg sodium, 209mg potassium

ORECCHIETTE AND CAVATELLI

The foods of Apulia are known for their simplicity and lack of pretension. Pasta from this region of Italy, made from the area's golden durum wheat, is a simple flour-and-water dough that is then hand-shaped, using the simplest of kitchen tools.

The following two pastas, although made from the same semolina dough, have a totally different texture and appearance, because of their shapes. Orecchiette, or little ears, are small pieces of dough that are flattened to form concave, earlike disks of pasta. Cavatelli are small quill-shaped pastas that are easily shaped with the help of a knife. Both pastas are best served with chunky vegetable or meat sauces.

DRY INGREDIENTS

2 cups unbleached, all-purpose flour,
    sifted with
1 cup finely ground semolina flour (see
    Note)

LIQUID INGREDIENTS

¾ cup water, plus 2 to 3 tablespoons
    additional water as needed

Following the instructions given in your owner's manual, prepare and set up the pasta machine with the breadstick extruder die.

All ingredients must be at room temperature. Add the dry ingredients to the pasta machine mixing bowl. Switch the pasta machine on. Slowly pour the liquid ingredients through the feed tube. Mix for approximately 3 minutes, or until the dough appears to be coming together in soft, pea-sized crumbs.

Following the instructions given in your owner's manual, begin to extrude the dough. Cut off the first 2 to 3 inches extruded and discard. If the dough appears to be too dry, stop extruding and start mixing again. Add the additional water, a tablespoon at a time, until the dough is the right consistency. Let mix for 60 seconds. Continue to extrude.

As the pasta begins to come out, gently move it away from the machine. Cut with a sharp paring knife or scissors at 12-inch lengths. Place the extruded dough in a single layer on a clean kitchen cloth. Cover with another cloth so that the dough does not dry out.

NOTE: Semolina flour is available in most specialty-food stores or from mail-order catalogues.

Hand-Shaping Orecchiette: Cut extruded dough, one strip at a time, into ½-inch pieces. Place a piece of dough in the palm of your hand. Flatten with your thumb, rotating the dough so that while you are flattening it you are also forcing it to become concave, with slightly thicker edges.

ORECCHIETTE

1. *Cut extruded dough into ½-inch pieces.*

2. *Place a piece of dough in the palm of your hand and flatten it with your thumb. Rotate the dough with your thumb against your palm so that it becomes concave, with slightly thicker edges.*

(continued)

Hand-Shaping Cavatelli: Cut extruded dough, one strip at a time, into ½-inch pieces. With your fingertips, gently roll the dough pieces into 1¼-inch-long cylinders. Flatten slightly with a butter knife. Place the blade of the knife lengthwise in the center of each cavatello and gently fold the sides onto the blade. Slide the blade out. The ends should curl slightly. If the cavatelli should open, gently pinch the ends.

CAVATELLI

1. Cut extruded dough in ½-inch pieces.

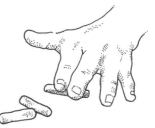

2. Gently roll the pieces of dough into 1¼-inch-long cylinders.

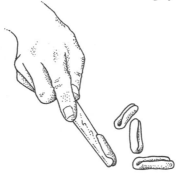

3. Slightly flatten the pieces of dough with a butter knife. Place the blade of the knife lengthwise in the center of the cavatelli and gently fold the sides onto the blade. Slide the blade out.

Place the orecchiette or cavatelli on a wire rack or a clean kitchen cloth. Let sit for 30 minutes before cooking, or store for later use (page 23).

FOUR **4**-OUNCE SERVINGS

RECOMMENDED SAUCES AND DISHES: Tomato Sauce (page 96), Sicilian Stuffed Meat Roll with Tomato Sauce (page 106), Veal Ragù and Wild Mushroom Sauce (page 108), Amatriciana Sauce (page 110), Broccoli and Onion Sauce (orecchiette only) (page 114), Broccoli di Rape and Sausage (page 115), Sun-Dried Tomato and Pasta Salad (page 124), and Moroccan Charmoula and Pasta Salad (page 125). Orecchiette also goes very well with these soups: Pasta and Beans (page 137), Pasta and Peas (page 140).

APPROXIMATE NUTRITIONAL ANALYSIS PER SERVING WITHOUT SAUCE

378 calories, 12g protein, 78g carbohydrates, 74g complex carbohydrates, 1g fat, 0mg cholesterol, 27mg sodium, 144mg potassium

POTATO GNOCCHI

Gnocchi are a very simple dumplinglike pasta made with simple ingredients like potatoes and flour. Unfortunately, gnocchi fall into two categories: light and very good or heavy and terrible.

The key to making good gnocchi is in the mixture. The cooked potatoes must be passed through a ricer or a food mill. This way they do not become mashed and mix well with the flour and other ingredients. I also find that by baking the potatoes rather than boiling them, the dough is drier and easier to work with.

DRY INGREDIENTS

1½ cups unbleached, all-purpose flour,
    sifted
1¼ pounds russet or Idaho potatoes
    (approximately five 4-ounce potatoes),
    baked until tender in a conventional
    oven or microwave
½ teaspoon salt

LIQUID INGREDIENTS

1 large egg, lightly beaten

Cut the hot baked potatoes in half. Scoop out and pass the potato through a ricer or food mill. Let cool to room temperature.

Following the instructions given in your owner's manual, prepare and set up the pasta machine with the gnocchi extruder die.

All ingredients must be at room temperature. Add the dry ingredients to the pasta machine mixing bowl. Switch the pasta machine on. Slowly pour the liquid ingredients through the feed tube. Mix for approximately 2 minutes, or until the dough appears to be coming together in soft balls.

Following the instructions given in your owner's manual, begin to extrude the dough. Cut off the first 2 to 3 inches extruded and discard. As the gnocchi begin to come out, cut in ½-inch lengths with a sharp paring knife. Place gnocchi on a lightly floured tray in a single layer. You will have to work fast, since the gnocchi usually extrude quickly. Sprinkle lightly with flour. If the gnocchi are uncurling, carefully recurl and pinch closed.

Cook immediately in batches by dropping with a slotted spoon into a 6-quart pot of boiling salted water. Gnocchi are done cooking when they rise and float on top of the water. Remove with a slotted spoon and drain in a colander.

FOUR 6-OUNCE SERVINGS

RECOMMENDED SAUCES AND DISHES: Tomato Sauce (page 96), Bolognese Tomato and Meat Sauce (page 104), Sicilian Stuffed Meat Roll with Tomato Sauce (page 106), Veal Ragù and Wild Mushroom Sauce (page 108), Butter and Sage Sauce (page 122), Pesto Sauce (page 123)

APPROXIMATE NUTRITIONAL ANALYSIS PER SERVING WITHOUT SAUCE

217 calories, 6g protein, 44g carbohydrates, 40g complex carbohydrates, 1g fat, 43mg cholesterol, 196mg sodium, 414mg potassium

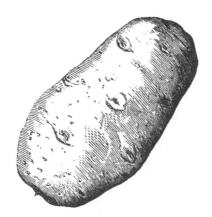

BASIC EGG AND FLAVORED PASTAS

Fresh egg pasta has been increasing in popularity over the past few years and is now readily available in most supermarket refrigerator cases. Homemade egg pasta, however, has a particular flavor and texture that make it outshine all others.

Egg pasta is slightly different in texture and flavor from the more simple durum-wheat and whole-grain pastas, being somewhat more subtle in texture. Traditionally made at home, it is almost always prepared and eaten fresh. It can also take on different flavors and colors through the addition of vegetable purées like spinach and carrot, or a delicate aroma from the addition of spices or finely minced herbs.

Egg pasta is the basis for an endless variety of shapes of fresh pasta. Made with simple, readily available ingredients, egg pasta is usually cut into flat noodlelike shapes, but it can also be extruded into any shape desired.

Basic Egg Pasta
(Pasta all'uovo)

The key to making perfect egg pasta is the appropriate dry to liquid ratio, which is approximately 1 cup flour to ¼ cup liquid. Keeping in mind that egg is a liquid and that one large egg is approximately ¼ cup liquid, use only large eggs for consistency.

DRY INGREDIENTS

3 cups unbleached, all-purpose flour,
  sifted
¾ teaspoon salt

LIQUID INGREDIENTS

3 large eggs, lightly beaten with
1½ teaspoons extra-virgin olive oil

Following the instructions given in your owner's manual, prepare and set up the pasta machine with an extruder die to make the desired shape of pasta.

All ingredients must be at room temperature. Place the liquid ingredients in a glass measuring cup. If less than ¾ cup, add some water to make up the balance.

Add the dry ingredients to the pasta machine mixing bowl. Switch the pasta machine on. Slowly pour the liquid ingredients through the feed tube. Mix for approximately 3 minutes, or until the dough appears to be coming together in soft pea-sized crumbs.

Following the instructions given in your owner's manual, begin to extrude the dough. Cut off the first 2 to 3 inches extruded and discard. As the pasta begins to come out, gently move it away from the machine. Cut with a sharp paring knife or scissors at desired lengths. Place extruded pasta on a wire rack or on a clean kitchen cloth. Let sit for at least 30 minutes before cooking, or store for later use (page 23).

FOUR 4-OUNCE SERVINGS

RECOMMENDED SAUCES: Fresh egg pasta is universal and can be served with any type of sauce or accompaniment.

APPROXIMATE NUTRITIONAL ANALYSIS PER SERVING WITHOUT SAUCE

424 calories, 15g protein, 72g carbohydrates, 68g complex carbohydrates, 7g fat, 192mg cholesterol, 459mg sodium, 156mg potassium

CHOLESTEROL-FREE PASTA

For those individuals who are on a cholesterol-free or reduced-cholesterol diet, egg substitutes and an electric pasta machine make "egg" pasta a reality. This pasta can be extruded or cut into any shape desired. You can also reduce the amount of egg substitute by ¼ cup and add an equal amount of strained carrots or beets.

DRY INGREDIENTS

3 cups unbleached, all-purpose flour, sifted
¾ teaspoon salt

LIQUID INGREDIENTS

¾ cup, less 1 tablespoon liquid egg
   substitute, blended with
1 tablespoon extra-virgin olive oil

Following the instructions given in your owner's manual, prepare and set up the pasta machine with an extruder die to make the desired shape of pasta.

All ingredients must be at room temperature. Place the liquid ingredients in a glass measuring cup.

Add the dry ingredients to the pasta machine mixing bowl. Switch the pasta machine on. Slowly pour the liquids through the feed tube. Mix for approximately 3 minutes, or until the dough appears to be coming together in soft pea-sized crumbs.

Following the instructions given in your owner's manual, begin to extrude the dough. Cut off the first 2 to 3 inches extruded and discard. As the pasta begins to come out, gently move it away from the machine. Cut with a sharp paring knife or scissors at desired lengths. Place extruded pasta on a wire rack or on a clean kitchen cloth. Let sit for at least 30 minutes before cooking, or store for later use (page 23).

FOUR 4-OUNCE SERVINGS

RECOMMENDED SAUCES: Cholesterol-free pasta is universal and can be served with any type of sauce or accompaniment.

APPROXIMATE NUTRITIONAL ANALYSIS PER SERVING WITHOUT SAUCE

407 calories, 15g protein, 72g carbohydrates, 67g complex carbohydrates, 6g fat, 0mg cholesterol, 478mg sodium, 242mg potassium

HERB- AND SPICE-FLAVORED EGG PASTAS

Basic egg-based pasta dough can be radically transformed by the simple addition of spices and fresh and dried herbs. The following recipes are a few suggestions of how to use ingredients from your herb garden, pantry, or greengrocer to add flavor and color to the homemade pasta you are making. The pasta dough can be extruded or shaped as desired.

1 recipe Basic Egg Pasta (page 49)

Prepare the Basic Egg Pasta recipe. Add the desired herbs or spices as indicated in the following variations.

ALL RECIPES MAKE FOUR 4-OUNCE SERVINGS.

BLACK PEPPER PASTA
(Pasta al Pepe)

Some people just cannot seem to get enough of the pungent flavor of black pepper. One of the earliest spices used by man, freshly ground black pepper adds complexity to the taste of fresh egg pasta.

Add ½ to 1 teaspoon freshly ground black pepper along with the dry ingredients. For best results, pepper should be medium ground.

RECOMMENDED SAUCES: Fresh Uncooked Tomato Sauce (page 98), Marinara Sauce (page 99), Puttanesca Sauce (page 100), Roasted Vegetable Sauce (page 116), Garlic and Olive Oil Sauce (page 121)

APPROXIMATE NUTRITIONAL ANALYSIS PER SERVING WITHOUT SAUCE
424 calories, 15g protein, 72g carbohydrates, 68g complex carbohydrates, 7g fat, 193mg cholesterol, 459mg sodium, 156mg potassium

SAFFRON PASTA
(Pasta Gialla)

Saffron is the gold of the spice world. Besides imparting a rich, golden hue to food, ounce for ounce it is even more expensive than gold. Fortunately for us, a very small amount goes a long way. When saffron is added to pasta dough, the yellow color intensifies. The flavor of the saffron is complemented by cream-based sauces, seafood, and mushrooms.

Add ½ teaspoon saffron threads, slightly crushed, to the liquid ingredients. Let saffron dissolve in the liquid approximately 15 minutes before adding to the pasta machine.

RECOMMENDED SAUCES: Tomato and Cream Sauce (page 97), Bolognese Tomato and Meat Sauce (page 104), Primavera Sauce (page 118), Wild Mushroom Sauce (page 119), Butter and Sage Sauce (page 122)

APPROXIMATE NUTRITIONAL ANALYSIS PER SERVING WITHOUT SAUCE

424 calories, 15g protein, 72g carbohydrates, 68g complex carbohydrates, 7g fat, 193mg cholesterol, 459mg sodium, 156mg potassium

GARLIC-AND-PARSLEY PASTA
(Pasta al Aglio e Prezzemolo)

Of all the herbs favored in Italian cookery, parsley is by far the most commonly used. This emerald-green herb slowly releases its flavor and aroma when cooked. When it is combined with garlic, the two flavors blend together to create a natural harmony.

Add ¼ cup finely minced fresh parsley and 5 cloves garlic, finely minced, along with the dry ingredients. For best results, use only Italian (flat-leaf) parsley.

RECOMMENDED SAUCES AND DISHES: Fresh Uncooked Tomato Sauce (page 98), Marinara Sauce (page 99), Puttanesca Sauce (page 100), Seafood Sauce (page 111), Roasted Vegetable Sauce (page 116), Wild Mushroom Sauce (page 119). Also try when making Sun-Dried Tomato and Pasta Salad (page 124).

APPROXIMATE NUTRITIONAL ANALYSIS PER SERVING WITHOUT SAUCE

432 calories, 16g protein, 74g carbohydrates, 68g complex carbohydrates, 7g fat, 193mg cholesterol, 464 mg sodium, 211 mg potassium

MINT PASTA
(Pasta alla Menta)

Surprisingly, mint is a staple of cooking in the Mediterranean basin. Used to flavor meats, vegetables, and sauces, mint adds a subtle flavor to pasta that ultimately complements certain dishes like no other herb.

Add ½ cup finely minced fresh mint along with the dry ingredients in the pasta machine.

RECOMMENDED SAUCES AND DISHES: Salmon and Lemon Sauce (page 113), Zucchini with Garlic and Olive Oil (page 120). Also try using when making Moroccan Charmoula and Pasta Salad (page 125).

APPROXIMATE NUTRITIONAL ANALYSIS PER SERVING WITHOUT SAUCE

424 calories, 15g protein, 72g carbohydrates, 68g complex carbohydrates, 7g fat, 193mg cholesterol, 459mg sodium, 156mg potassium

SPINACH PASTA
(PASTA VERDE)

Of all the flavored pastas, spinach is without doubt the most popular. Homemade spinach pasta is easy to make using finely chopped frozen spinach.

Spinach pasta dough can also be used for making hand-cut noodles like tagliatelle (page 69), maltagliati (page 80), pappardelle (page 68), and farfalle (page 81). Simply use the lasagne extruder die and follow the appropriate instructions for making the type of pasta desired.

DRY INGREDIENTS

3 cups unbleached, all-purpose flour,
    sifted
5 ounces frozen chopped spinach,
    cooked, cooled, and squeezed dry
½ teaspoon salt

LIQUID INGREDIENTS

2 large eggs, lightly beaten with
1 tablespoon water
1½ teaspoons extra-virgin olive oil

Following the instructions given in your owner's manual, prepare and set up the pasta machine with an extruder die to make the desired shape of pasta.

All ingredients must be at room temperature. Add the dry ingredients to the pasta machine mixing bowl, making sure to crumble the spinach over the flour. Switch the pasta machine on. Slowly pour the liquid ingredients through the feed tube. Mix for approximately 3 minutes, or until the dough appears to be coming together in soft pea-sized crumbs.

Following the instructions given in your owner's manual, begin to extrude the dough. Cut off the first 2 to 3 inches extruded and discard. As the pasta begins to come out, gently move it away from the machine. Cut with a sharp paring knife or scissors at desired lengths. Place extruded pasta on a wire rack or on a clean kitchen cloth. Let sit for at least 30 minutes before cooking, or store for later use (page 23).

FOUR 4-OUNCE SERVINGS

RECOMMENDED SAUCES: Tomato Sauce (page 96), Sunday Meat Sauce (page 102), Bolognese Tomato and Meat Sauce (page 104), Clam Sauce (page 112), Primavera Sauce (page 118), Wild Mushroom Sauce (page 119), Butter and Sage Sauce (page 122)

APPROXIMATE NUTRITIONAL ANALYSIS PER SERVING WITHOUT SAUCE

411 calories, 15g protein, 74g carbohydrates, 68g complex carbohydrates, 6g fat, 129mg cholesterol, 337mg sodium, 242mg potassium

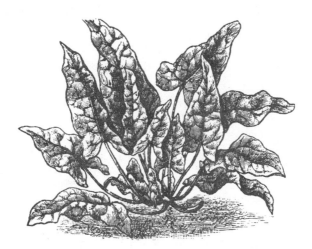

TOMATO PASTA
(PASTA ROSSA)

To enjoy the flavor of tomato pasta fully, never serve it with a tomato-base sauce. Instead, couple it with an interesting sauce that contrasts in both color and flavor, such as pesto sauce or garlic-and-olive-oil sauce. You can even extrude it in small interesting shapes to be used later to make macaroni salad.

DRY INGREDIENTS

3 cups unbleached, all-purpose flour, sifted
½ teaspoon salt

LIQUID INGREDIENTS

2 large eggs, lightly beaten with
2 tablespoons tomato paste
1½ teaspoons extra-virgin olive oil

Following the instructions given in your owner's manual, prepare and set up the pasta machine with an extruder die to make the desired shape of pasta.

All ingredients must be at room temperature. Place the liquid ingredients in a glass measuring cup. If less than ¾ cup, add some water to make up the balance.

Add the dry ingredients to the pasta machine mixing bowl. Switch the pasta machine on. Slowly pour the liquid ingredients through the feed tube. Mix for approximately 3 minutes, or until the dough appears to be coming together in soft pea-sized crumbs.

Following the instructions given in your owner's manual, begin to extrude the dough. Cut off the first 2 to 3 inches extruded and discard. As the pasta begins to come out, gently move it away from the machine. Cut with a sharp paring knife or scissors at desired lengths. Place extruded pasta on a wire rack or on a clean kitchen cloth. Let sit for at least 30 minutes before cooking, or store for later use (page 23).

FOUR 4-OUNCE SERVINGS

RECOMMENDED SAUCES AND DISHES: Clam Sauce (page 112), Primavera Sauce (page 118), Garlic and Olive Oil Sauce (page 121), Pesto Sauce (page 123). Also try in Sun-Dried Tomato and Pasta Salad (page 124).

APPROXIMATE NUTRITIONAL ANALYSIS PER SERVING WITHOUT SAUCE

408 calories, 14g protein, 74g carbohydrates, 68g complex carbohydrates, 6g fat, 129mg cholesterol, 371mg sodium, 213mg potassium

CARROT PASTA

(PASTA ARANCIA)

A wonderful shade of golden orange, carrot pasta is a cheery addition to anyone's repertoire of pasta recipes.

DRY INGREDIENTS

3 cups unbleached, all-purpose flour, sifted
¾ teaspoon salt

LIQUID INGREDIENTS

2 large eggs, lightly beaten with
1 large carrot, cut into chunks, boiled, and
   puréed (approximately ¼ cup purée), or
   one 4-ounce jar strained baby-food
   carrots
2 teaspoons extra-virgin olive oil

Following the instructions given in your owner's manual, prepare and set up the pasta machine with an extruder die to make the desired shape of pasta.

All ingredients must be at room temperature. Place the liquid ingredients in a glass measuring cup. If less than ¾ cup, add some water to make up the balance.

Add the dry ingredients to the pasta machine mixing bowl. Switch the pasta machine on. Slowly pour the liquid ingredients through the feed tube. Mix for approximately 3 minutes, or until the dough appears to be coming together in soft pea-sized crumbs.

Following the instructions given in your owner's manual, begin to extrude the dough. Cut off the first 2 to 3 inches extruded and discard. As the pasta begins to come out, gently move it away from the machine. Cut with a sharp paring knife or scissors at desired lengths. Place extruded pasta on a wire rack or on a clean kitchen cloth. Let sit for at least 30 minutes before cooking, or store for later use (page 23).

FOUR 4-OUNCE SERVINGS

RECOMMENDED SAUCES: Tomato Sauce (page 96), Garlic and Olive Oil Sauce (page 120), Butter and Sage Sauce (page 122), Pesto Sauce (page 123)

APPROXIMATE NUTRITIONAL ANALYSIS PER SERVING WITHOUT SAUCE

419 calories, 14g protein, 75g carbohydrates, 68g complex carbohydrates, 6g fat, 129mg cholesterol, 458mg sodium, 201mg potassium

BEET PASTA
(PASTA ROSA)

Even though you probably have never eaten beet pasta, with its attractive pink hue, these unique noodles from the part of Italy that borders with Austria make for a sensational combination when served with sauces that accentuate their color, especially salmon and lemon sauce.

DRY INGREDIENTS

3 cups unbleached, all-purpose flour,
   sifted
3/4 teaspoon salt

LIQUID INGREDIENTS

2 large eggs, lightly beaten with
1 large beet, cut into chunks, boiled, and
   puréed (approximately 1/4 cup purée), or
   one 4-ounce jar strained baby-food
   beets
1 teaspoon extra-virgin olive oil

Following the instructions given in your owner's manual, prepare and set up the pasta machine with an extruder die to make the desired shape of pasta.

All ingredients must be at room temperature. Place the liquid ingredients in a glass measuring cup. If less than 3/4 cup, add some water to make up the balance.

Add the dry ingredients to the pasta machine mixing bowl. Switch the pasta machine on. Slowly pour the liquid ingredients through the feed tube. Mix for approximately 3 minutes, or until the dough appears to be coming together in soft pea-sized crumbs.

Following the instructions given in your owner's manual, begin to extrude the dough. Cut off the first 2 to 3 inches extruded and discard. As the pasta begins to come out, gently move it away from the machine. Cut with a sharp paring knife or scissors at desired lengths. Place extruded parts on a wire rack or on a clean kitchen cloth. Let sit for at least 30 minutes before cooking, or store for later use (page 23).

FOUR 4-OUNCE SERVINGS

RECOMMENDED SAUCES: Salmon and Lemon Sauce (page 113), Zucchini with Garlic and Olive Oil (page 120), Garlic and Olive Oil Sauce (page 121), Butter and Sage Sauce (page 122), Pesto Sauce (page 123)

APPROXIMATE NUTRITIONAL ANALYSIS PER SERVING WITHOUT SAUCE

408 calories, 14g protein, 75g carbohydrates, 68g complex carbohydrates, 5g fat, 129mg cholesterol, 462mg sodium, 223mg potassium

PESTO PASTA
(PASTA AL PESTO)

Pesto is a favorite accompaniment to pasta, and as such it can also add flavor and color when mixed into the dough.

Since pesto pasta is so rich in flavor, it can be served simply with some ricotta and grated Parmesan cheese or with any of the sauces given.

DRY INGREDIENTS
3 cups unbleached, all-purpose flour, sifted

LIQUID INGREDIENTS
2 large eggs, lightly beaten with
¼ cup Pesto Sauce (page 123)

Following the instructions given in your owner's manual, prepare and set up the pasta machine with an extruder die to make the desired shape of pasta.

All ingredients must be at room temperature. Place the liquid ingredients in a glass measuring cup. If less than ¾ cup, add some water to make up the balance.

Add the dry ingredients to the pasta machine mixing bowl. Switch the pasta machine on. Slowly pour the liquid ingredients through the feed tube. Mix for approximately 3 minutes, or until the dough appears to be coming together in soft pea-sized crumbs.

Following the instructions given in your owner's manual, begin to extrude the dough. Cut off the first 2 to 3 inches extruded and discard. As the pasta begins to come out, gently move it away from the machine. Cut with a sharp paring knife or scissors at desired lengths. Place extruded pasta on a wire rack or on a clean kitchen cloth. Let sit for at least 30 minutes before cooking, or store for later use (page 23).

FOUR 4-OUNCE SERVINGS

RECOMMENDED SAUCES: Fresh Uncooked Tomato Sauce (page 98), Zucchini with Garlic and Olive Oil (page 120), Garlic and Olive Oil Sauce (page 121)

APPROXIMATE NUTRITIONAL ANALYSIS PER SERVING WITHOUT SAUCE
447 calories, 15g protein, 73g carbohydrates, 68g complex carbohydrates, 10g fat, 133mg cholesterol, 86mg sodium, 162mg potassium

LEMON PASTA
(PASTA AL LIMONE)

Lemon pasta is an unknown entity in Italy. Nevertheless, I personally enjoy the fresh lemon flavor that shines through when this pasta is served with a light seafood or vegetable sauce.

DRY INGREDIENTS
3 cups unbleached, all-purpose flour, sifted
1 teaspoon finely grated lemon rind
$\frac{1}{2}$ teaspoon salt

LIQUID INGREDIENTS
2 large eggs, lightly beaten with
$\frac{1}{4}$ cup freshly squeezed lemon juice

Following the instructions given in your owner's manual, prepare and set up the pasta machine with an extruder die to make the desired shape of pasta.

All ingredients must be at room temperature. Place the liquid ingredients in a glass measuring cup. If less than $\frac{3}{4}$ cup, add some water to make up the balance.

Add the dry ingredients to the pasta machine mixing bowl. Switch the pasta machine on. Slowly pour the liquid ingredients through the feed tube. Mix for approximately 3 minutes, or until the dough appears to be coming together in soft pea-sized crumbs.

Following the instructions given in your owner's manual, begin to extrude the dough. Cut off the first 2 to 3 inches extruded and discard. As the pasta begins to come out, gently move it away from the machine. Cut with a sharp paring knife or scissors at desired lengths. Place extruded pasta on a wire rack or on a clean kitchen cloth. Let sit for at least 30 minutes before cooking, or store for later use (page 23).

FOUR 4-OUNCE SERVINGS

RECOMMENDED SAUCES AND DISHES: Clam Sauce (page 112), Salmon and Lemon Sauce (page 113), Zucchini with Garlic and Olive Oil (page 120), Garlic and Olive Oil Sauce (page 121). Also try using in Moroccan Charmoula and Pasta Salad (page 125).

APPROXIMATE NUTRITIONAL ANALYSIS PER SERVING WITHOUT SAUCE
390 calories, 14g protein, 73g carbohydrates, 68g complex carbohydrates, 4g fat, 129mg cholesterol, 307mg sodium, 156mg potassium

HAND-CUT AND STUFFED PASTAS

THE EMILIA-ROMAGNA REGION of Italy is renowned for its wonderful hand-cut and stuffed pastas made from fine, thin sheets of rich egg dough. Served with sauces or in broth and soups, these pastas may require a bit more attention and care, yet they are definitely worth it.

From small hat-shaped cappelletti to wide-noodle pappardelle, the pastas in this chapter can be made well in advance and then frozen. When accompanied by a wonderful tomato, meat, or wild mushroom sauce, these pastas will transform even the novice cook into a first-rate pasta maker, or as they say in Italian, a *sfoglina*.

HAND-CUT EGG PASTA
(PASTA SFOGLIA)

While this delicate, egg-enriched pasta, traditionally used as the wrapping for delectable meat, cheese, and vegetable fillings, is usually hand-kneaded and then rolled out paper-thin, the following recipe achieves the same results while saving some time by using the pasta machine.

DRY INGREDIENTS

3 cups unbleached, all-purpose flour, sifted

LIQUID INGREDIENTS

3 large eggs, lightly beaten with
1 large egg yolk (reserve the egg white)
1½ teaspoons extra-virgin olive oil

Following the instructions given in your owner's manual, prepare and set up the pasta machine with the lasagne extruder die.

All ingredients must be at room temperature. Place the liquid ingredients in a glass measuring cup. If less than ¾ cup, add some of the reserved egg white to make up the balance.

Add the dry ingredients to the pasta machine mixing bowl. Switch the pasta machine on. Slowly pour the liquid ingredients through the feed tube. Mix for approximately 3 minutes, or until the dough appears to be coming together in soft pea-sized crumbs.

Following the instructions given in your owner's manual, begin to extrude the dough. Cut off the first 2 to 3 inches extruded and discard. As the pasta begins to come out, gently move it away from the machine. Cut with a sharp paring knife or scissors at the length specified in the recipe you are making. Place the extruded pasta on a clean kitchen cloth. Cover with another cloth so the extruded dough does not dry out.

Proceed with the hand-shaping instructions from any of the following recipes in this chapter.

LASAGNE
(BROAD NOODLES)

When extruded from the pasta machine, lasagne are too thick to provide good results when baked with cheese and sauce. By simply rolling out the extruded dough you can easily stretch it thin enough, achieving excellent results.

1 recipe Hand-Cut Egg Pasta (page 65)

Using the lasagne extruder die, extrude the dough in 6-inch strips. Cover with a clean kitchen cloth so the dough does not dry out. Using a rolling pin or a hand-cranked pasta maker set on a $^1/_{16}$-inch setting, roll out the dough as thin as possible. Stack the dough pieces one on top of the other in piles of four. Using a ruler and a sharp knife, square off the edges. Discard the scraps. Proceed with the recipe for Baked Lasagne (page 129).

8 SERVINGS

APPROXIMATE NUTRITIONAL ANALYSIS PER SERVING WITHOUT SAUCE

218 calories, 8g protein, 36g carbohydrates, 34g complex carbohydrates, 4g fat, 123mg cholesterol, 31mg sodium, 79mg potassium

MANICOTTI AND CANNELLONI

Manicotti and cannelloni are thin tubes of pasta dough stuffed with a cheese or meat filling. They are simple to make and will be a family favorite.

Since the dough extruded from the pasta machine is too narrow, it is necessary to join together 2 dough strips to make up the appropriate width of the dough.

1 recipe Hand-Cut Egg Pasta (page 65)

Using the lasagne extruder die, extrude the dough in 5-inch lengths. Cover with a clean kitchen cloth so that the dough does not dry out. Place 2 pieces of dough on a clean work surface, overlapping the long edges slightly. Dip your index finger in a small bowl of water and lightly wet the seam. Sprinkle lightly with flour. Using a rolling pin, roll out the dough as thin as possible while joining the pieces together. Turn the dough over. Lightly wet the seam with water, sprinkle with flour, and roll gently with a rolling pin. Place on a large plate and cover with another clean cloth. Continue until all dough is used.

Stack the pasta sheets one on top of the other in piles of four. Square off the edges with a sharp knife and cut each pile into 5-by-4-inch rectangles. Discard any scraps. Cover with a clean cloth and let rest for 30 minutes before boiling. Proceed with either the recipe for Baked Manicotti (page 130) or Baked Cannelloni (page 130).

APPROXIMATELY 18 SHELLS

APPROXIMATE NUTRITIONAL ANALYSIS PER SHELL

98 calories, 4g protein, 16g carbohydrates, 15g complex carbohydrates, 2g fat, 56mg cholesterol, 14mg sodium, 35mg potassium

PAPPARDELLE

(CUT CURLY NOODLES)

Pappardelle are substantial noodles that are best served with a rich meat or vegetable sauce. Much wider than most other pastas, pappardelle are cut with a fluted pastry wheel to give them their customary curly edges.

1 recipe Hand-Cut Egg Pasta (page 65)

Using the lasagne extruder die, extrude the dough in 4-inch strips. Cover with a clean kitchen cloth so the dough does not dry out. Using a rolling pin or hand-cranked pasta maker set on a $1/16$-inch setting, roll out the dough as thin as possible. Stack the dough strips one on top of the other in piles of four. Using a ruler and a fluted pastry wheel, square off the edges. Discard the scraps. Cut each dough pile in half lengthwise. Cut each half-piece in half. Place the pappardelle on a wire rack or a clean kitchen cloth. Let sit for 30 minutes before cooking, or store for later use (page 23).

FOUR 3-OUNCE SERVINGS

RECOMMENDED SAUCES: Tomato Sauce (page 96), Bolognese Tomato and Meat Sauce (page 104), Veal Ragù and Wild Mushroom Sauce (page 108), Wild Mushroom Sauce (page 119)

APPROXIMATE NUTRITIONAL ANALYSIS PER SERVING WITHOUT SAUCE

439 calories, 16g protein, 72g carbohydrates, 67g complex carbohydrates, 8g fat, 246mg cholesterol, 61mg sodium, 159mg potassium

TAGLIATELLE
(HAND-CUT NOODLES)

Tagliatelle are a specialty of Bologna and are typically served with that region's tomato and meat sauce.

The name *tagliatelle* comes from the Italian verb *tagliare*, "to cut," since the dough is usually rolled by hand and then cut into strips. Tagliatelle are simple to make once you have made the dough in the pasta machine.

1 recipe Hand-Cut Egg Pasta (page 65)

Using the lasagne extruder die, extrude the dough in 6-inch strips. Cover with a clean kitchen cloth so the dough does not dry out. Using a rolling pin or a hand-cranked pasta maker set on a $^{1}/_{16}$-inch setting, roll out the dough as thin as possible. Stack the dough pieces one on top of the other in piles of four. Using a ruler and a sharp knife, square off the edges. Discard the scraps.

Using a ruler as a guide, cut each dough pile into $^{1}/_{2}$-inch-wide strips. Let sit uncovered for 30 minutes before cooking, or store for later use (page 23).

FOUR 3-OUNCE SERVINGS

RECOMMENDED SAUCES: Tomato Sauce (page 96), Tomato and Cream Sauce (page 97), Bolognese Tomato and Meat Sauce (page 104), Primavera Sauce (page 118), Butter and Sage Sauce (page 122)

APPROXIMATE NUTRITIONAL ANALYSIS PER SERVING WITHOUT SAUCE

438 calories, 16g protein, 72g carbohydrates, 67g complex carbohydrates, 8g fat, 246mg cholesterol, 61mg sodium, 158mg potassium

RAVIOLI

If you have never eaten fresh homemade ravioli, you are in for a real treat. These ravioli will outshine anything you have ever eaten in the past.

FILLING

¾ cup ricotta

¼ cup freshly grated Parmesan cheese

1 large egg, lightly beaten

1½ teaspoons finely minced fresh parsley

1 recipe Hand-Cut Egg Pasta (page 65)

Mix all the filling ingredients together in a medium-sized bowl. Set aside.

Using the lasagne extruder die, extrude the dough in 12-inch-long strips. Cover with a clean kitchen cloth so the dough does not dry out. Cut the dough strips into three 4-inch-long pieces. Using a rolling pin or a hand-cranked pasta maker set on a $^1/_{16}$-inch setting, roll out the dough pieces as thin as possible. Stack the dough pieces one on top of the other in piles of four. Using a ruler and a sharp knife, square off the edges. The dough should be at least 2¼ inches wide and 5 inches long. Discard the scraps.

Lay individual pieces of dough, 8 at a time, on a clean work surface. Fold each piece in half like a book and open. Drop a scant teaspoon of filling in the center of the bottom half of each piece of dough. Dip your index finger in a small bowl of water and wet the edges. Fold the top over the bottom. Squeeze the edges together to seal well, at the same time forcing the filling into the center. Place the ravioli on a wire rack or a clean kitchen cloth. Let sit for 30 minutes before cooking, or store for later use (page 23).

MAKES APPROXIMATELY **48** RAVIOLI (ABOUT **6** SERVINGS)

RECOMMENDED SAUCES: Tomato Sauce (page 96), Tomato and Cream Sauce (page 97), Sunday Meat Sauce (page 102), Bolognese Tomato and Meat Sauce (page 104), Butter and Sage Sauce (page 122), Pesto Sauce (page 123)

APPROXIMATE NUTRITIONAL ANALYSIS PER SERVING WITHOUT SAUCE

380 calories, 17g protein, 49g carbohydrates, 45g complex carbohydrates, 12g fat, 226mg cholesterol, 157mg sodium, 156mg potassium

RAVIOLI

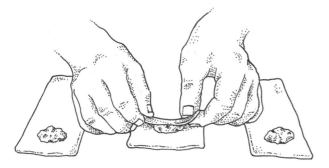

1. Place the filling in the center of the bottom portion of each piece of dough. Lightly dampen the edges with water. Fold the top of the dough over the bottom.

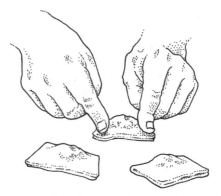

2. Squeeze the edges together to seal well, forcing the filling to the center.

TORTELLONI

(SPINACH-AND-CHEESE—STUFFED PASTA SQUARES)

Tortelloni are like large ravioli stuffed with a savory filling of spinach and ricotta. Although simple to prepare, they make a very impressive offering as a first course or as a light entrée.

FILLING

¾ cup ricotta

5 ounces chopped frozen spinach, cooked and well-drained

6 tablespoons freshly grated Parmesan cheese

1 large egg

¼ teaspoon salt

1 recipe Hand-Cut Egg Pasta (page 65)

Mix the filling ingredients together in a medium-sized bowl. Set aside.

Using the lasagne extruder die, extrude the dough in 5-inch strips. Cover with a clean kitchen cloth so the dough does not dry out. On a clean work surface, place 2 pieces of dough, overlapping the long edges slightly. Dip your finger in a small bowl of water and lightly wet the seam. Sprinkle lightly with flour. Using a rolling pin, roll out the dough as thin as possible while joining the 2 pieces together at the same time. Turn the dough over. Lightly wet the seam with water, sprinkle with flour, and roll gently with the rolling pin. Place the sheet on a large plate and cover with another clean cloth. Repeat with the remaining dough.

Stack the pasta sheets one on top of the other in piles of four. Square off the edges with a sharp knife and cut into 5-by-4-inch rectangles. Discard the scraps.

Lay individual dough, eight at a time, on the work surface. Fold each piece of dough in half like a book and open. Drop 2 teaspoons of filling in the center of the bottom half of each piece of dough. Dip your index finger in a small bowl of water and wet the edges. Fold the top over the bottom. Squeeze the edges together to seal well. Trim the 3 sealed edges with a fluted pastry wheel. Place the tortelloni on a wire rack or a clean kitchen cloth. Let sit for 30 minutes before cooking, or store for later use (page 23).

MAKES APPROXIMATELY 18 TORTELLONI (6 SERVINGS)

RECOMMENDED SAUCES: Tomato Sauce (page 96), Tomato and Cream Sauce (page 97), Butter and Sage Sauce (page 122)

TORTELLONI

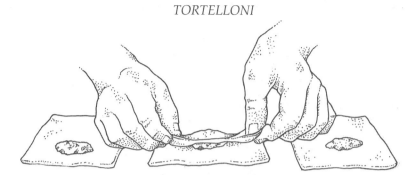

1. *Place the filling in the center of the bottom portion of each piece of dough. Lightly dampen the
   edges with water. Fold the top of the dough
   over the bottom.*

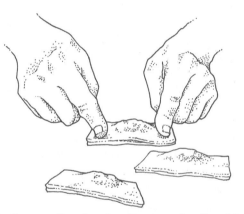

2. *Squeeze the edges together to seal well and trim
   the three sealed edges with a fluted pastry
   wheel.*

APPROXIMATE NUTRITIONAL ANALYSIS PER SERVING WITHOUT SAUCE
396 calories, 19g protein, 51g carbohydrates, 46g complex carbohydrates, 13g fat, 227mg
cholesterol, 305mg sodium, 277mg potassium

TORTELLINI AND CAPPELLETTI

Although time-consuming to make, homemade tortellini and cappelletti are, without a doubt, worth the trouble. Nothing compares to the classical Bolognese dish of tortellini with tomato and meat sauce or cappelletti with freshly made chicken soup.

TORTELLINI
(Stuffed Pasta Rings)

FILLING

1 tablespoon sweet butter
2 ounces lean pork loin, cut into ½-inch cubes
2 ounces boneless chicken or turkey breast, cut into ½-inch cubes
1½ tablespoons finely minced mortadella

1½ tablespoons finely minced prosciutto
1 large egg
Pinch grated nutmeg
½ cup freshly grated Parmesan cheese

1 recipe Hand-Cut Egg Pasta (page 65)

In a large skillet heat the butter over medium heat. Add the cubed pork and chicken and sauté until just cooked. Place in a blender jar or food processor bowl with the remaining filling ingredients. Chop and blend the ingredients until just grainy in texture. Set aside.

Using the lasagne extruder die, extrude the dough in 12-inch-long strips. Cover with a clean kitchen cloth so the dough does not dry out. Cut the dough into 2½-inch-long pieces. Using a rolling pin, roll out each dough piece as thin as possible. The pieces should be 2¾ to 3 inches wide.

Cut the dough pieces into 2½-inch circles with a biscuit cutter or a small glass. Drop a scant ½ teaspoon of filling in the center of each circle. Fold in half and squeeze the edges together to seal. Hold the tortellino between your thumb and index finger. Fold it around your finger and bring the two ends together. Press tightly to seal and fold down the curved top to form a cuff. Place the tortellini on a wire rack or a clean kitchen towel. Let sit for 30 minutes before cooking, or store for later use (page 23).

MAKES APPROXIMATELY 80 TORTELLINI (5 SERVINGS)

TORTELLINI

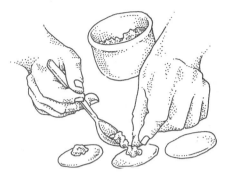

1. Place the filling in the center of each circle of dough.

2. Fold the circle of dough in half and squeeze the edges together to seal.

3. Hold the tortellino between your thumb and index finger.

4. Fold the ends around your index finger and press tightly to seal together.

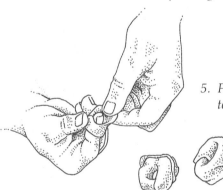

5. Fold down the curved top to form a cuff.

APPROXIMATE NUTRITIONAL ANALYSIS PER SERVING WITHOUT SAUCE

532 calories, 29g protein, 59g carbohydrates, 54g complex carbohydrates, 19g fat, 294mg cholesterol, 474mg sodium, 268mg potassium

CAPPELLETTI
(Stuffed Little Hats)

FILLING

¾ cup ricotta
¾ cup freshly grated Parmesan cheese
1 large egg, lightly beaten
1½ teaspoons finely minced fresh parsley

Pinch freshly ground black pepper
Pinch grated nutmeg

1 recipe Hand-Cut Egg Pasta (page 65)

In a medium-sized bowl blend together the filling ingredients. Set aside.

Using the lasagne extruder die, extrude the dough into 12-inch-long strips. Place the strips of dough on a lightly floured work surface. Cover with a clean kitchen cloth so the dough does not dry out. Cut the dough into 2-inch-long pieces. Using a rolling pin, roll out each piece as thin as possible. Stack one on top of the other in piles of four. Using a ruler and a sharp knife, square off the edges. Discard the scraps. The dough pieces should be 2 to 3 inches square.

Place the pieces of dough, 8 at a time, on a clean work surface. Drop ½ teaspoon of filling in the center of each square. Dip your index finger in a small bowl of water and moisten the edges. Fold the cappelletti in half diagonally to form a triangle. Squeeze the edges together to seal well. Bring the 2 bottom points of the triangle together and pinch to join. Bend the top point back slightly. Place the cappelletti on a wire rack or a clean kitchen cloth. Let sit for 30 minutes before cooking, or store for later use (page 23).

MAKES APPROXIMATELY 72 CAPPELLETTI (6 SERVINGS)

APPROXIMATE NUTRITIONAL ANALYSIS PER SERVING WITHOUT SAUCE

419 calories, 21g protein, 50g carbohydrates, 45g complex carbohydrates, 14g fat, 232mg cholesterol, 312mg sodium, 166mg potassium

RECOMMENDED SAUCES AND DISHES FOR TORTELLINI AND CAPPELLETTI: Tomato Sauce (page 96), Tomato and Cream Sauce (page 97), Bolognese Tomato and Meat Sauce (page 104), Butter and Sage Sauce (page 122). Also try with Chicken Soup (page 136).

CAPPELLETTI

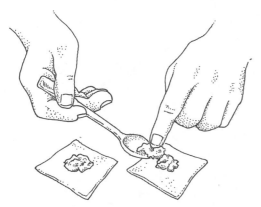

1. Place the filling in the center of each square of dough.

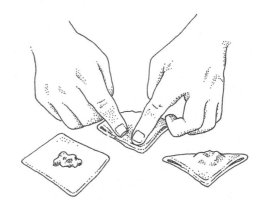

2. Lightly dampen the edges with water and fold in half diagonally to form a triangle. Squeeze the edges together to seal well.

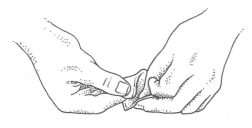

3. Bring the two bottom points of the triangle together and pinch to join.

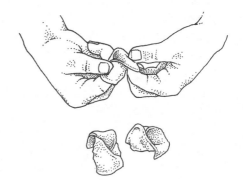

4. Bend the top point back slightly.

AGNOLOTTI DI MELANZANE
(EGGPLANT-STUFFED HALF-MOONS)

Eggplant is a versatile vegetable that appears in numerous guises in Mediterranean cooking. It is very popular in southern Italy, especially in Calabria and Sicily, where it is used as a stuffing for agnolotti, delicious half-moons of pasta stuffed with a flavorful eggplant-and-cheese filling.

FILLING

1 small eggplant (approximately 8 ounces)
¾ cup ricotta
2 tablespoons freshly grated Pecorino
  Romano cheese, plus extra for serving
1½ tablespoons finely minced fresh basil

1 tablespoon finely minced fresh parsley
¼ teaspoon salt
Pinch freshly ground black pepper

1 recipe Hand-Cut Egg Pasta (page 65)

Preheat the broiler. Prick the eggplant a few times with a fork. Place on a baking sheet under the broiler. Turn periodically so that the eggplant roasts evenly. When it feels soft and tender, remove from the broiler. Cut in half and discard the seeds. Scoop out the flesh and let drain in a colander. Once drained, chop fine and mix with the other filling ingredients in a medium-sized mixing bowl. Set aside.

Using the lasagne extruder die, extrude the dough in 12-inch-long strips. Cover with a clean kitchen cloth so the dough does not dry out. Cut the dough into 2½-inch-wide pieces. Using a rolling pin or a hand-cranked pasta maker set on a ¹⁄₁₆-inch setting, roll out each piece as thin as possible. The pieces should be 2¾ to 3 inches square.

Cut the dough into 2½-inch circles with a biscuit cutter or small glass. Discard the scraps. Drop a scant ½ teaspoon of filling in the center of each circle. Fold in half and squeeze the edges together to seal well. Place the agnolotti on a wire rack or a clean kitchen cloth. Let sit for 30 minutes before cooking, or store for later use (page 23).

To serve the agnolotti, spoon sufficient sauce on the bottom of a dinner plate just to cover. Place the cooked agnolotti on the dish and spoon additional sauce on top. Serve with freshly grated Pecorino Romano cheese.

MAKES APPROXIMATELY 60 AGNOLOTTI (4 SERVINGS)

RECOMMENDED SAUCES: Tomato Sauce (page 96), Tomato and Cream Sauce (page 97), Marinara Sauce (page 99), Roasted Vegetable Sauce (page 116), Butter and Sage Sauce (page 122)

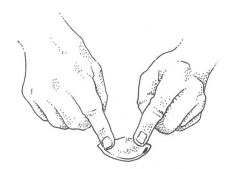

1. Place the filling in the center of each circle of dough.

2. Fold the circle of dough in half and squeeze the edges together to seal well.

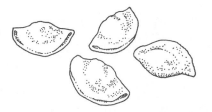

APPROXIMATE NUTRITIONAL ANALYSIS PER SERVING WITHOUT SAUCE

570 calories, 25g protein, 78g carbohydrates, 67g complex carbohydrates, 17g fat, 337mg cholesterol, 291mg sodium, 377mg potassium

MALTAGLIATI
(FREE-FORM NOODLES)

Although usually made with dough scraps left over from making pastas such as tortellini and ravioli, maltagliati are also made when the cook is in a rush and does not have time to cut the pasta dough into perfect strips. You see, *male tagliati* means "poorly cut" in Italian, which is exactly how these noodles look.

1 recipe Hand-Cut Egg Pasta (page 65)

Using the lasagne extruder die, extrude the dough in 4-inch strips. Cover with a clean kitchen cloth so the dough does not dry out. Using a rolling pin or a hand-cranked pasta maker set on a $\frac{1}{16}$-inch setting, roll out the dough as thin as possible. Stack the dough pieces one on top of the other in piles of four. Using a ruler and sharp knife, square off the edges.

Using a long, sharp knife, cut each dough pile diagonally in varying widths ranging from $\frac{1}{4}$ to $\frac{1}{2}$ inch wide. Place the maltagliati on a wire rack or clean kitchen cloth. Let sit for 30 minutes before cooking, or store for later use (page 23).

FOUR 4-OUNCE SERVINGS

RECOMMENDED SAUCES AND DISHES: Tomato Sauce (page 96), Tomato-Onion-Basil Sauce (page 101), Salmon and Lemon Sauce (page 113), Wild Mushroom Sauce (page 119), Butter and Sage Sauce (page 122). Also serve with Chicken Soup (page 136).

APPROXIMATE NUTRITIONAL ANALYSIS PER SERVING WITHOUT SAUCE

438 calories, 16g protein, 72g carbohydrates, 67g complex carbohydrates, 8g fat, 246mg cholesterol, 61mg sodium, 159mg potassium

FARFALLE
(BUTTERFLIES)

There are as many different types of pastas as there are shapes and sizes. One of my favorites is the easy-to-make farfalle, or butterflies, recognizable by their characteristic bow-tie shape.

1 recipe Hand-Cut Egg Pasta (page 65)

Using the lasagne extruder die, extrude the dough in 4-inch strips. Cover with a clean kitchen cloth so the dough does not dry out. Using a rolling pin or a hand-cranked pasta maker set on a $\frac{1}{16}$-inch setting, roll out the dough as thin as possible. Stack the dough pieces one on top of the other in piles of four. Using a ruler and a fluted pastry wheel, square off the edges. Discard the scraps. The dough pieces should be approximately 5 to 6 inches long and 3 inches wide.

Using a fluted pastry wheel, cut each dough pile at $1\frac{1}{2}$-inch intervals along its 6-inch length so you wind up with pieces that are approximately $1\frac{1}{2}$ by 3 inches. Take each piece of the cut dough and pinch the long edges to the center so that a bow-tie shape is formed. Let sit uncovered on a wire rack or clean kitchen cloth for 30 minutes before cooking, or store for later use (page 23).

FOUR 3-OUNCE SERVINGS

RECOMMENDED SAUCES AND DISHES: Tomato Sauce (page 96), Tomato and Cream Sauce (page 97), Bolognese Tomato and Meat Sauce (page 104), Primavera Sauce (page 118), Wild Mushroom Sauce (page 119), Butter and Sage Sauce (page 122), Pesto Sauce (page 123), Sun-Dried Tomato and Pasta Salad (page 124), Moroccan Charmoula and Pasta Salad (page 125)

APPROXIMATE NUTRITIONAL ANALYSIS PER SERVING WITHOUT SAUCE

438 calories, 16g protein, 12g carbohydrates, 67g complex carbohydrates, 8g fat, 246mg cholesterol, 61mg sodium, 158mg potassium

ASIAN NOODLES

NOODLES HOLD AN IMPORTANT PLACE in the Asian culture and diet. Either stir-fried with meats, seafood, and vegetables, added to soups, or shaped into dumplings, Asian noodles are a good source of nutrients. With the exception of fried noodles, most Asian noodle dishes are low in fat and high in complex carbohydrates.

While we are most familiar with the traditional wheat and egg noodles, other forms made from rice and buckwheat are also very popular. Asian noodles are available dried in some specialty shops, but a pasta machine and the right ingredients enable you to have a ready supply of fresh Chinese egg noodles, Southeast Asian rice noodles, and Japanese buckwheat soba whenever the mood strikes.

WON TON SKINS
(YUN TUN P'I)

Won ton is Chinese for "cloud bird." When properly made, they should be light and airy, not chewy like pasta.

The secret to making a perfect won ton is in the dough. By using bread flour, which is higher in gluten than all-purpose flour, you will be able to get the dough to stretch as thin as possible. This versatile dough is also used to make other Chinese dumplings.

DRY INGREDIENTS

3 cups bread flour, sifted
2 teaspoons salt

LIQUID INGREDIENTS

2 large eggs, lightly beaten with
¼ cup water

Cornstarch for rolling out dough

Following the instructions given in your owner's manual, prepare and set up the pasta machine with the lasagne extruder die.

All ingredients must be at room temperature. Place the liquid ingredients in a glass measuring cup. If less than ¾ cup, add some more water to make up the balance.

Add the dry ingredients to the pasta machine mixing bowl. Switch the pasta machine on. Slowly pour the liquid ingredients through the feed tube. Mix for approximately 3 minutes, or until the dough appears to be coming together in soft pea-sized crumbs.

Following the instructions given with your owner's manual, begin to extrude the dough. Cut off the first 2 to 3 inches extruded and discard. As the dough begins to come out, gently move it away from the machine. Cut with a sharp paring knife or scissors at 4-inch lengths. Place the extruded dough on a wire rack or on a clean kitchen cloth. Cover with another cloth so the extruded dough does not dry out.

Lightly sprinkle cornstarch on a clean work surface. Lay dough pieces on top, one at a time. Sprinkle lightly with cornstarch. With a rolling pin, roll out each piece until it is at least 3 inches wide and paper thin. With a ruler and a sharp knife, square off the edges

(continued)

and cut the dough into 3-inch squares. Discard the scraps. Lightly sprinkle the squares with cornstarch and stack one on top of the other. Place on a clean kitchen cloth. Cover with another cloth so the won ton skins do not dry out. Let sit for 30 minutes before using, or store for later use (page 23).

To make dough for Pot Stickers (page 156) and Shrimp Beggar's Purses (page 158), follow the same procedure as outlined above; however, cut the dough into 3-inch circles, using a biscuit cutter or a glass.

APPROXIMATELY 60 WON TON SKINS

RECOMMENDED USES: Won Tons (page 154), Pot Stickers (page 156), Beggar's Purses (page 158)

APPROXIMATE NUTRITIONAL ANALYSIS PER WON TON SKIN

26 calories, 1g protein, 5g carbohydrates, 9g complex carbohydrates, 0g fat, 9mg cholesterol, 75mg sodium, 9mg potassium

CHINESE EGG NOODLES
(HSEEN HSYEN DON MYEN)

In parts of China far from the rice-growing regions, wheat and other grains provide the starch and carbohydrates necessary for a well-balanced diet. As in most Asian cultures, noodles play an important role in helping to extend other, more expensive ingredients into a nutritious meal.

The following recipe for egg noodles can be extruded as thin as angel-hair pasta for such dishes as Filipino stir-fried egg noodles or as wide as linguine for lo mein. Because of its high gluten content, bread flour resembles the type of wheat flour used in Asia in noodle making and provides the best results.

DRY INGREDIENTS

3 cups bread flour, sifted   1 teaspoon salt

LIQUID INGREDIENTS

2 large eggs, lightly beaten with
¼ cup water

Following the instructions given in your owner's manual, prepare and set up the pasta machine with an extruder die to make the desired shape of pasta. Use the angel-hair, spaghetti, or linguine extruder dies when making Asian noodles.

All ingredients must be at room temperature. Place the liquid ingredients in a glass measuring cup. If less than ¾ cup, add some water to make up the balance.

Add the dry ingredients to the pasta machine mixing bowl. Switch the pasta machine on. Slowly pour the liquid ingredients through the feed tube. Mix for approximately 3 minutes, or until the dough appears to be coming together in soft, pea-sized crumbs.

Following the instructions given in your owner's manual, begin to extrude the dough. Cut off the first 2 to 3 inches extruded and discard. As the pasta begins to come out, gently move it away from the machine. Cut with a sharp paring knife or scissors at desired lengths. Place extruded pasta on a wire rack or on a clean kitchen cloth. Sprinkle lightly with flour and gently toss with your fingers so that the noodles do not stick together. Let sit for at least 30 minutes before cooking, or store for later use (page 23).

FOUR 4-OUNCE SERVINGS

(*continued*)

RECOMMENDED DISHES: Lo Mein (page 146), Pan-Fried Noodles with Chicken (page 150), Cold Sesame Noodles and Chicken (page 152), Filipino Stir-Fried Egg Noodles (page 166)

APPROXIMATE NUTRITIONAL ANALYSIS PER SERVING OF NOODLES ONLY

387 calories, 14g protein, 72g carbohydrates, 67g complex carbohydrates, 9g fat, 128mg cholesterol, 572mg sodium, 137mg potassium

RICE NOODLES
(MEE FUN)

Rice noodles are enjoyed in most Asian countries. Since rice does not have any gluten, it is not kneaded and then extruded as are wheat noodles. In Asia, rice flour is mixed with water, spread in thin layers, and steamed until the dough has set. The dough is then cut into the desired shapes and lengths. Without sacrificing flavor and texture, homemade rice noodles can be made by mixing the rice flour with high-gluten bread flour.

The following recipe for rice noodles can be extruded as thin as angel hair for such dishes as Cantonese Rice noodles with Beef or as wide as linguine for Thai Rice Noodles with Broccoli.

DRY INGREDIENTS

1¾ cups bread flour, sifted with
1¼ cups white rice flour

LIQUID INGREDIENTS

¾ cup water

Following the instructions given in your owner's manual, prepare and set up the pasta machine with an extruder die to make the desired shape of pasta. Use the angel-hair, spaghetti, or linguine extruder dies when making Asian noodles.

All ingredients must be at room temperature. Add the dry ingredients to the pasta machine mixing bowl. Switch the pasta machine on. Slowly pour the liquid ingredients through the feed tube. Mix for approximately 3 minutes, or until the dough appears to be coming together in soft, pea-sized crumbs.

Following the instructions given in your owner's manual, begin to extrude the dough. Cut off the first 2 to 3 inches extruded and discard. As the pasta begins to come out, gently move it away from the machine. Cut with a sharp paring knife or scissors at desired lengths. Place the extruded pasta on a wire rack or on a clean kitchen cloth. Sprinkle lightly with flour and gently toss with your fingers so that the noodles do not stick together. Let sit for at least 30 minutes before cooking, or store for later use (page 23).

FOUR 4-OUNCE SERVINGS

(continued)

RECOMMENDED DISHES: Cantonese Rice Noodles with Beef (page 148), Curried Singapore Rice Noodles (page 163), Thai Rice Noodles with Broccoli (page 165), Stir-Fried Thai Rice Noodles (page 168)

APPROXIMATE NUTRITIONAL ANALYSIS PER SERVING OF NOODLES ONLY

380 calories, 9g protein, 81g carbohydrates, 39g complex carbohydrates, 1g fat, 0mg cholesterol, 2mg sodium, 96mg potassium

JAPANESE BUCKWHEAT NOODLES
(SOBA)

Japanese buckwheat noodles are delicate compared with other Asian noodles made from wheat flour and, sometimes, eggs. Buckwheat flour is milled from the seeds of this wild meadow plant. Since it is not a grain, it does not have any gluten and therefore will not extrude well when made into dough in a pasta machine. The way to overcome this is to mix the buckwheat flour with high-gluten bread flour. The result is excellent.

DRY INGREDIENTS

1¾ cups bread flour, sifted with
¾ cup light buckwheat flour

LIQUID INGREDIENTS

¾ cup plus 1 teaspoon water

Following the instructions given in your owner's manual, prepare and set up the pasta machine with the spaghetti extruder die.

All ingredients must be at room temperature. Add the dry ingredients to the pasta machine mixing bowl. Switch the pasta machine on. Slowly pour the liquid ingredients through the feed tube. Mix for approximately 3 minutes, or until the dough appears to be coming together in soft, pea-sized crumbs.

Following the instructions given in your owner's manual, begin to extrude the dough. Cut off the first 2 to 3 inches extruded and discard. As the pasta begins to come out, gently move it away from the machine. Cut with a sharp paring knife or scissors at desired lengths. Place the extruded pasta on a wire rack or on a clean kitchen cloth. Sprinkle lightly with flour and gently toss with your fingers so that the noodles do not stick together. Let sit for at least 30 minutes before cooking, or store for later use (page 23).

FOUR 4-OUNCE SERVINGS

RECOMMENDED DISHES: Japanese Soba in Broth (page 143)

APPROXIMATE NUTRITIONAL ANALYSIS PER SERVING, NOODLES ONLY

261 calories, 8g protein, 55g carbohydrates, 50g complex carbohydrates, 1g fat, 0mg cholesterol, 5mg sodium, 166mg potassium

PART TWO

RECIPES FOR USING FRESH PASTAS AND NOODLES

SAUCES AND SALADS

BAKED PASTAS

SOUPS

ASIAN NOODLES, DUMPLINGS, AND SAUCES

DESSERTS AND BREADSTICKS

SAUCES AND SALADS

Now that you have made your delicious, fresh homemade pasta, it would be a shame to serve it with mediocre, store-bought, jarred sauce. Sauces and accompaniments should always be simple and natural to let the texture and flavor of the pasta shine through.

Some of the following recipes, like marinara sauce and garlic-and-olive-oil sauce, can be made in less than thirty minutes from start to finish while you are making and cooking the pasta. Other recipes, like Sunday meat sauce, may require a little planning beforehand. All of the sauces can also be made well in advance and frozen for later use. All sauce recipes can be doubled if desired.

When making sauces with canned tomatoes, I prefer using whole, peeled plum tomatoes packed in their own juice. If you can only find those packed in tomato juice, add ½ cup water to the recipe to dilute the juice. To strain tomatoes, pass through a food mill or force by hand through a colander. Always discard any skin, seeds, or fibers that remain, since these will make the sauce bitter-tasting.

TOMATO SAUCE

(SUGO DI POMODORO)

It is almost inconceivable that it was not until the nineteenth century that tomatoes began to become a mainstay in Italian cooking. This very simple, meatless tomato sauce is rich in flavor and goes well with all types of fresh egg pastas and stuffed and baked dishes like lasagne, manicotti, and cannelloni.

4 tablespoons extra-virgin olive oil
1 small yellow onion, finely minced
1 small carrot, finely minced
1 stalk celery, finely minced
3 cups canned plum tomatoes,
   finely strained, with their juice

1 teaspoon salt
1/8 teaspoon freshly ground black pepper
1 teaspoon finely chopped fresh parsley

1 pound pasta, cooked al dente
Freshly grated Parmesan cheese for
   serving

In a medium saucepan heat the olive oil. Add the onion. Sauté over low heat, for 5 to 8 minutes, until transparent. Stir frequently so the onions do not brown. Add the carrot and celery. Cook for 5 minutes, stirring frequently.

Add the tomatoes, salt, and pepper. Bring to a boil. Lower the heat. Let the sauce simmer for 45 minutes, stirring occasionally. Remove from the heat and stir in parsley. Add salt and pepper to taste.

Serve over pasta with Parmesan cheese or use to prepare baked pasta dishes.

4 SERVINGS

RECOMMENDED PASTAS AND DISHES: All types of egg pasta, including hand-cut noodles and also cornmeal and buckwheat pasta. Try serving with gnocchi and stuffed pastas or when making baked pasta dishes.

APPROXIMATE NUTRITIONAL ANALYSIS PER SERVING OF SAUCE

164 calories, 2g protein, 10g carbohydrates, 1g complex carbohydrates, 14g fat, 0mg cholesterol, 836mg sodium, 459mg potassium

Ziti (page 33 or 38) with Amatriciana Sauce (page 110).

Egg, Spinach, and Carrot Fettuccine (pages 49, 54, and 57) with Wild Mushroom Sauce (page 119).

◄   *Potato Gnocchi (page 44) with Bolognese Tomato and Meat Sauce (page 104).*

Seafood Stew with Noodles (page 138).

Chicken Soup with Noodles (page 136).

Clockwise from left: Honey Mustard Sauce (page 161), Chili Sauce (page 162), Ginger Sauce (page 161), Shrimp Beggar's Purses (page 158), Curried Singapore Rice Noodles (page 163), Won Tons (page 155), and Pot Stickers (page 156).

TOMATO AND CREAM SAUCE
(SALSA ROSA)

This wonderfully rich tomato sauce is well suited to stuffed pastas like tortelloni and cannelloni. The slow cooking of the vegetables adds a velvetlike quality and richness to the flavor and texture of the sauce.

2 tablespoons unsalted butter
2 tablespoons extra-virgin olive oil
1 small carrot, finely minced
1 stalk celery, finely minced
1 small yellow onion, finely minced
3 cups canned plum tomatoes, finely
   strained, with their juice

1 teaspoon salt
½ cup heavy cream

1 pound pasta, cooked al dente
Freshly grated Parmesan cheese for
   serving

In a medium-sized saucepan heat the butter and olive oil over medium heat. Add the carrot, celery, and onion. Sauté over low heat, 5 to 8 minutes, until soft. Stir frequently so the vegetables do not brown. Add the tomatoes and salt. Bring to a boil. Lower the heat and let the sauce simmer for 45 minutes. Add the cream and stir to blend. Let simmer for 2 minutes more. Taste for salt.

Place a small pool of sauce on a dinner plate. Lay some pasta on top and cover lightly with additional sauce. Serve with grated Parmesan cheese.

4 SERVINGS

RECOMMENDED PASTAS: All types of stuffed pastas; also, any egg pasta

APPROXIMATE NUTRITIONAL ANALYSIS PER SERVING OF SAUCE
175 calories, 2g protein, 8g carbohydrates, 0.4g complex carbohydrates, 16g fat, 38mg cholesterol, 569mg sodium, 350mg potassium

Raspberry Crisp (page 174).

FRESH UNCOOKED TOMATO SAUCE

(SUGO DI POMODORO CRUDO)

Only garden-ripened tomatoes or those bought from a farm stand will work in this recipe. The tomatoes have to be very fresh and ripe. The quintessential summer pasta sauce!

2 pounds sun-ripened plum tomatoes
2 cloves garlic, peeled and crushed
4 sprigs fresh basil, lightly crushed to
    release flavor
2 teaspoons salt

⅓ cup extra-virgin olive oil

1 pound pasta, cooked al dente
Freshly grated Parmesan cheese

Plunge the tomatoes in a large pot of boiling water. Remove with a slotted spoon after 30 seconds. Peel the tomatoes, discard the seeds, and chop coarsely.

Place the chopped tomatoes in a large glass or ceramic bowl. Add the remaining sauce ingredients and mix together. Cover the bowl with a dinner plate and let sit at room temperature for 2 to 4 hours. Taste for salt.

Serve over pasta with freshly grated Parmesan cheese.

4 SERVINGS

RECOMMENDED PASTAS: Durum-wheat angel-hair pasta or spaghetti

APPROXIMATE NUTRITIONAL ANALYSIS PER SERVING OF SAUCE

207 calories, 2g protein, 11g carbohydrates, 1g complex carbohydrates, 19g fat, 0mg cholesterol, 1086mg sodium, 513mg potassium

MARINARA SAUCE

(SALSA ALLA MARINARA)

One of the most basic of tomato sauces, *salsa alla marinara*, or "sailor's sauce," is thought to have been created by mariners who wanted a robust tomato sauce that could be quickly prepared from readily available ingredients.

3 tablespoons extra-virgin olive oil
6 cloves garlic, peeled and crushed
4 cups canned plum tomatoes, seeded
   and coarsely chopped, with their juice
2 teaspoons salt
½ teaspoon freshly ground black pepper

2 sprigs fresh basil
1 tablespoon finely chopped fresh parsley

1 pound pasta, cooked al dente
Freshly grated Parmesan cheese for
  serving

In a large saucepan heat the olive oil and garlic over medium heat. When the garlic starts to sizzle, pour in the tomatoes. Add the salt, pepper, and basil. Bring to a boil and lower the heat. Let the sauce simmer for 30 minutes, stirring occasionally. Remove from the heat, stir in the parsley, and taste for salt and pepper.

Serve over pasta with Parmesan cheese.

4 SERVINGS

RECOMMENDED PASTAS: Durum-wheat spaghetti or linguine or cornmeal pasta

APPROXIMATE NUTRITIONAL ANALYSIS PER SERVING OF SAUCE

145 calories, 3g protein, 12g carbohydrates, 2g complex carbohydrates, 11g fat, 0mg cholesterol, 1458mg sodium, 558mg potassium

PUTTANESCA SAUCE
(SALSA ALLA PUTTANESCA)

This flavorful, easy-to-prepare sauce heralds from Naples. Rumor has it that it was first developed by the Neapolitan ladies of the evening to provide some quick nourishment while on the job.

3 tablespoons extra-virgin olive oil
3 cloves garlic, coarsely chopped
3 anchovy fillets, finely chopped
3 cups canned plum tomatoes, seeded and coarsely chopped, with their juice
¼ teaspoon crushed red pepper
1 tablespoon small capers, well rinsed under water and drained

⅓ cup pitted oil-cured black olives
1 teaspoon salt
2 tablespoons finely chopped fresh parsley

1 pound pasta, cooked al dente
Fresh grated Pecorino Romano cheese for serving

In a large saucepan heat the olive oil over medium heat. Add the garlic. Sauté over low heat for 1 to 2 minutes or until the garlic just starts to turn golden. Stir frequently so the garlic does not brown. Add the chopped anchovies and mash together with the garlic. Add the tomatoes, crushed red pepper, capers, olives, and salt. Stir to combine. Bring to a boil. Lower the heat. Let the sauce simmer for 15 minutes. Add the parsley and taste for salt and pepper.

Serve over pasta with Pecorino Romano cheese.

4 SERVINGS

RECOMMENDED PASTAS: Durum-wheat or garlic-and-parsley spaghetti or linguine

APPROXIMATE NUTRITIONAL ANALYSIS PER SERVING OF SAUCE

149 calories, 3g protein, 9g carbohydrates, 1g complex carbohydrates, 12g fat, 3mg cholesterol, 1010mg sodium, 435mg potassium

TOMATO-ONION-BASIL SAUCE
(SUGO DI CIPOLLE)

The following recipe has always been a personal favorite. The mellow flavor of the slow-cooked onions blends with the tomato to produce a thick, flavorful sauce enhanced by the fragrance of the fresh basil.

4 tablespoons extra-virgin olive oil
1 pound yellow onions (about 4 medium), peeled, halved, and thinly sliced
4 cups canned plum tomatoes, finely strained, with their juice
8 large fresh basil leaves

2 teaspoons salt
¼ teaspoon freshly ground black pepper

1 pound pasta, cooked al dente
Freshly grated Parmesan cheese for serving

In a medium-sized saucepan heat the olive oil. Add the onions and sauté over low heat, 8 to 10 minutes, until transparent. Stir frequently so the onions do not brown.

Add the tomatoes, basil, salt, and pepper. Bring to a boil. Lower the heat and let the sauce simmer for 45 minutes, stirring periodically. Taste for salt and pepper.

Serve over pasta with Parmesan cheese.

4 SERVINGS

RECOMMENDED PASTAS: Durum-wheat pasta, such as penne or ziti; or hand-cut egg pasta, such as pappardelle, maltagliati, or farfalle

APPROXIMATE NUTRITIONAL ANALYSIS PER SERVING OF SAUCE
211 calories, 4g protein, 20g carbohydrates, 1g complex carbohydrates, 14g fat, 0mg cholesterol, 1460mg sodium, 713mg potassium

SUNDAY MEAT SAUCE
(RAGÙ)

There is probably no greater mainstay in the Italian-American kitchen than the ever-popular Sunday sauce. In hundreds of thousands of households, Sunday just wouldn't be Sunday without the slowly simmering pot of tomato sauce on top of the stove. This is the Lacalamita version.

4 tablespoons extra-virgin olive oil
1 pound neck bones or pork ribs, trimmed
    of all excess fat
4 links sweet or hot Italian sausage
1 medium yellow onion, finely minced
12 meatballs (recipe follows)
9 cups canned plum tomatoes (three 28-
    ounce cans), finely strained, with juice

3 sprigs fresh basil
4 teaspoons salt
½ teaspoon freshly ground black pepper

2 pounds pasta, cooked al dente
Freshly grated Pecorino Romano cheese
    for serving

In an 8-quart saucepan heat the olive oil over high heat. Add the neck bones or ribs. Cook until evenly browned on all sides and remove from the pot. Add the sausages and brown, then remove these from the pot. Pour out all but 3 tablespoons of oil and lower the heat. Add the onion. Sauté, stirring frequently so the onion does not brown. Add the neck bones, sausages, and meatballs.

Add the tomatoes, basil, salt, and pepper. Raise the heat and bring to a boil. Lower the heat and let the sauce simmer for 1½ hours, stirring periodically. Taste for salt and pepper.

Serve the sauce with meatballs over pasta, sprinkling on Pecorino Romano cheese.

MEATBALLS

1 pound lean ground beef
2 large eggs
½ cup plain bread crumbs
2 tablespoons finely minced fresh parsley
4 tablespoons freshly grated Pecorino
    Romano cheese

1 teaspoon salt
⅛ teaspoon freshly ground black pepper
Vegetable oil for frying

In a large mixing bowl blend together all the ingredients except oil. Do not overmix. Shape into 8 meatballs. In a large skillet heat ½ inch of oil over medium heat. Add the meatballs and fry evenly until browned on all sides. Remove with a slotted spoon and drain on paper toweling.

8 SERVINGS

RECOMMENDED PASTAS AND DISHES: All shapes of durum-wheat pasta. Also use for lasagne or other baked pasta dishes

APPROXIMATE NUTRITIONAL ANALYSIS PER SERVING OF SAUCE AND MEATS

669 calories, 46g protein, 18g carbohydrates, 5g complex carbohydrates, 46g fat, 220mg cholesterol, 2295mg sodium, 1137mg potassium

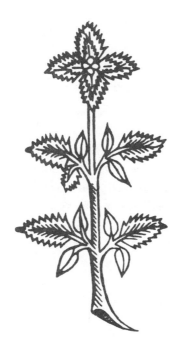

BOLOGNESE TOMATO AND MEAT SAUCE
(RAGÙ ALLA BOLOGNESE)

This rich Italian meat sauce is the traditional accompaniment to tagliatelle, Italian egg noodles, or tortellini—those wonderful, small pillows of pasta stuffed with meat or cheese.

The secret to a perfect *ragù alla Bolognese* is slow simmering so that the sauce thickens as the flavors blend together. Be sure to chop the vegetables very fine. A food processor is good for this.

4 tablespoons extra-virgin olive oil
½ cup finely chopped yellow onions
⅔ cup finely chopped carrots
⅔ cup finely chopped celery
2 ounces prosciutto, finely minced
1 pound lean ground beef
1½ teaspoons salt
¼ teaspoon freshly ground black pepper
¼ teaspoon freshly grated nutmeg

1¼ cups milk
4 cups canned plum tomatoes, finely strained, with their juice
1 sprig fresh basil

1 pound pasta, cooked al dente
Freshly grated Parmesan cheese for serving

In a large saucepan heat the olive oil. Add the onions. Sauté over low heat, 5 to 8 minutes, until transparent. Stir frequently so the onions do not brown. Add the carrots, celery, and prosciutto. Cook for 5 minutes, stirring frequently.

Raise the heat to high and add the meat. Mix the meat and vegetables until well combined. Cook, stirring frequently, just until the meat loses its pink color. Break up any large pieces with the spoon. Add the salt, pepper, and nutmeg, then the milk. Stir to blend. Bring to a boil. Lower the heat and simmer the sauce until most of the milk has evaporated.

Add the tomatoes and basil. Bring to a boil. Lower the heat and let simmer for 1¾ hours, stirring periodically. Taste for salt and pepper.

Serve over pasta with grated Parmesan cheese.

4 SERVINGS

RECOMMENDED PASTAS: Potato gnocchi, tagliatelle, all types of egg pasta, including hand-cut and stuffed pasta such as tortellini or ravioli

APPROXIMATE NUTRITIONAL ANALYSIS PER SERVING OF SAUCE

390 calories, 27g protein, 12g carbohydrates, 1g complex carbohydrates, 26g fat, 89mg cholesterol, 1041mg sodium, 820mg potassium

Sicilian Stuffed Meat Roll with Tomato Sauce

(Farsumagrù con Sugo)

Farsumagrù, the quintessential Sicilian meat dish of rolled beef fillet stuffed with meat and cheese, is delicious served with gnocchi or cavatelli on the side.

Do not be put off by the long list of ingredients. Farsumagrù is simple to make and will become a family favorite.

8 ounces lean ground beef
1 large egg
½ cup freshly grated Parmesan cheese
¼ teaspoon salt
¼ teaspoon freshly ground black pepper
1½ pounds fillet of beef for braciole or a large piece of flank steak, pounded thin
½ cup bread crumbs

4 slices boiled ham
1 small yellow onion, halved and thinly sliced
2 tablespoons finely minced fresh parsley
2 ounces provolone cheese, cut into long, thin strips
3 tablespoons extra-virgin olive oil

SAUCE

1 tablespoon extra-virgin olive oil
1 small yellow onion, finely chopped
1 medium carrot, finely minced
1 stalk celery, finely minced
⅔ cup red wine
2 cups canned plum tomatoes, coarsely strained, with their juice

1 cup water
1½ teaspoons salt
⅛ teaspoon freshly ground black pepper

1 pound pasta, cooked al dente

Combine the ground beef, egg, Parmesan cheese, salt, and pepper in a small bowl. Place the fillet of beef on a clean work surface with the widest edge pointing toward you. Sprinkle with the bread crumbs, ½ inch from the edges. Cover with the ham slices, overlapping if necessary. Carefully spread the ground beef mixture on top of the ham by forming thin patties. Pat to make as flat and even as possible. Sprinkle with the onion and parsley and line the sliced provolone along the wide edge of the fillet closest to you, at least 1 inch from the edge.

Carefully roll up the fillet, jelly-roll fashion, starting with the long end closest to you. Be careful that the stuffing does not fall out. Finish with the seam facing down. Tightly tie up the ends of the roll with white kitchen string and thereafter at 2-inch intervals. Secure tightly, since the meat will shrink when cooked.

In a large Dutch oven or skillet with a tight-fitting cover, heat the olive oil. Brown the rolled fillet on all sides. Remove from the pan, place on a platter, and cover with foil. Prepare the sauce.

In the same pan the meat was browned in, heat the olive oil. Add the onion. Sauté over medium heat for 5 to 6 minutes. Stir frequently so the onions do not brown. Add the carrot and celery. Sauté for 5 minutes, stirring continuously. Add the wine. Scrape the pan to loosen any food particles. Bring to a boil and let the alcohol evaporate, approximately 5 minutes. Add the tomatoes, water, salt, and pepper. Stir together. Add the browned meat. Bring to a boil. Cover and let simmer for 1 to 1½ hours, turning the meat occasionally. The meat is ready when it can be easily pierced with a fork.

Remove the meat from the pan and let sit, covered, for 15 minutes. Remove the string and cut the meat into ½-inch slices. Place on a heated platter, overlapping slightly. Reheat the sauce and taste for salt and pepper. Spoon the sauce over sliced meat and pasta.

6 SERVINGS

RECOMMENDED PASTAS: Potato gnocchi, cavatelli, or egg farfalle; also, durum-wheat penne or ziti

APPROXIMATE NUTRITIONAL ANALYSIS PER SERVING OF SAUCE WITH MEAT
570 calories, 53g protein, 8g carbohydrates, 0.8g complex carbohydrates, 34g fat, 176mg cholesterol, 1359mg sodium, 968mg potassium

VEAL RAGÙ AND WILD MUSHROOM SAUCE

(SUGO DI CARNE E FUNGHI)

The following recipe is an adaptation of a personal favorite from Lidia Bastianich, renowned restaurateur and cookbook author. Full of the earthy flavors imparted by the dried porcini, this sauce is a perfect foil to potato gnocchi or wide noodles.

¾ ounce dried porcini mushrooms (see Note)
1 cup boiled water
½ cup all-purpose flour
1 teaspoon salt
⅛ teaspoon freshly ground black pepper
1½ pounds boneless lean veal, cut into ½-inch cubes
6 tablespoons extra-virgin olive oil
1 medium yellow onion, finely chopped
1 tablespoon tomato paste

3 medium bay leaves
⅓ cup dry white wine
3 cups chicken stock

1 pound pasta, cooked al dente
Freshly grated Parmesan cheese for serving

Soak the dried porcini for 20 minutes in the boiled water. With a slotted spoon remove the porcini from the water. Strain the soaking water to remove any dirt particles and set aside.

Put the flour in a bowl and season with the salt and pepper. Dredge the veal in the flour mixture. Shake off any excess. In a large skillet, heat 4 tablespoons of the olive oil over high heat. Add the veal cubes in batches and brown evenly on all sides over medium heat. Remove with a slotted spoon.

Place the remaining 2 tablespoons of olive oil in a large saucepan and sauté the chopped onion for 3 to 5 minutes or until transparent. Stir frequently so the onion does not brown. Add the tomato paste and cook for a minute, stirring continuously. Add the bay leaves, veal, and wine. Stir to mix. Add the porcini, the reserved soaking water, and the chicken stock. Bring to a boil. Lower the heat and let the sauce simmer, covered, for approximately 1 to 1½ hours, or until the veal is fork tender. Taste for salt and pepper.

Serve over pasta with grated Parmesan cheese.

6 SERVINGS

RECOMMENDED PASTAS: Potato gnocchi; fresh egg, cornmeal, or buckwheat pappardelle or farfalle

NOTE: Dried porcini mushrooms are available in most specialty-food stores or from mail-order catalogues.

APPROXIMATE NUTRITIONAL ANALYSIS PER SERVING OF SAUCE

514 calories, 38g protein, 10g carbohydrates, 8g complex carbohydrates, 34g fat, 134mg cholesterol, 858mg sodium, 495mg potassium

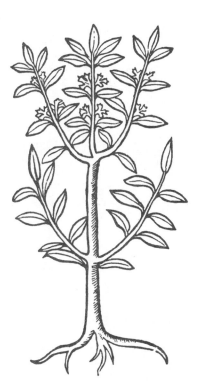

AMATRICIANA SAUCE
(PASTA ALL'AMATRICIANA)

This wonderfully piquant sauce is the specialty of the town of Amatrice, located northeast of Rome. Pancetta, an Italian bacon, is important to the success of this recipe and is available in most good Italian food stores. If you wish, you can modify, according to your personal taste, the amount of crushed red pepper called for in the recipe.

3 tablespoons extra-virgin olive oil
½ cup finely chopped yellow onion
2 ounces pancetta, finely diced
2 cups canned plum tomatoes, seeded, coarsely chopped, and drained of all juice
1 teaspoon salt
½ teaspoon crushed red pepper
¼ teaspoon freshly ground black pepper

1 pound pasta, cooked al dente
½ cup water reserved from cooking pasta
1 tablespoon finely chopped fresh parsley
2 tablespoons freshly grated Pecorino Romano cheese, plus additional for serving

In a large saucepan heat the olive oil. Add the onion. Sauté over medium heat for 5 to 6 minutes, or until the onion is a light golden color. Stir frequently so the onion does not brown. Add the pancetta and cook for 4 to 6 minutes, or until most of the fat has melted. Stir continuously so the onion and pancetta do not brown.

Add the tomatoes, salt, crushed red pepper, and black pepper. Stir to combine. Bring to a boil. Lower the heat. Let the sauce simmer for 15 minutes, stirring periodically. Taste for salt and pepper.

In a large serving bowl mix the drained pasta with the sauce, the reserved water, the parsley, and the 2 tablespoons of Pecorino Romano cheese. Serve with additional cheese on the side.

4 SERVINGS

RECOMMENDED PASTAS: Durum-wheat or cornmeal pasta, such as ziti or penne

APPROXIMATE NUTRITIONAL ANALYSIS PER SERVING OF SAUCE
218 calories, 7g protein, 7g carbohydrates, 1g complex carbohydrates, 18g fat, 15mg cholesterol, 1013mg sodium, 380mg potassium

SEAFOOD SAUCE
(SALSA FRA DIAVOLO)

When served over very thin angel-hair pasta, *salsa fra diavolo*, which translates literally as "sauce from the devil," is without a doubt a perfect balance between the celestial lightness of the pasta and the devilish spiciness of the sauce.

4 tablespoons extra-virgin olive oil
6 cloves garlic, peeled and crushed
3 cups canned plum tomatoes, seeded and coarsely chopped, with their juice
1½ teaspoons salt
1 teaspoon crushed red pepper

8 ounces small raw shrimp, peeled and deveined
8 ounces small raw scallops
1 tablespoon finely chopped fresh parsley

1 pound pasta, cooked al dente

In a large saucepan heat 2 tablespoons of the olive oil with the garlic over medium heat. When the garlic starts to sizzle, pour in the tomatoes. Add the salt and crushed red pepper. Bring to a boil. Lower the heat. Simmer the sauce for 30 minutes, stirring occasionally.

In a skillet heat the remaining 2 tablespoons of olive oil over high heat. Add the shrimp and scallops. Cook for about 2 minutes, or until the shrimp turn pink, stirring frequently. Add to the tomato sauce. Stir in the parsley. Cook for 3 to 4 minutes, or until the sauce just begins to bubble. Taste for salt.

Serve the sauce over pasta.

4 SERVINGS

RECOMMENDED PASTAS: Durum-wheat, angel-hair, or linguine

APPROXIMATE NUTRITIONAL ANALYSIS PER SERVING OF SAUCE
279 calories, 23g protein, 11g carbohydrates, 2g complex carbohydrates, 16g fat, 129mg cholesterol, 1326mg sodium, 683mg potassium

CLAM SAUCE
(SALSA ALLE VONGOLE)

As with clam chowder, there are two very basic and simple ways to prepare clam sauce: in a red tomato sauce or in the clam's own juices with white wine. While I prefer my chowder red, clam sauce is always served white in our home.

2 dozen littleneck clams, scrubbed clean
½ cup water
5 tablespoons extra-virgin olive oil
4 cloves garlic, coarsely chopped
¼ cup dry white wine
1 teaspoon salt

¼ teaspoon freshly ground black pepper
3 tablespoons finely chopped fresh
  parsley

1 pound pasta, cooked al dente

Place the clams and water in a large saucepan with a close-fitting lid. Steam open over high heat. Shake the pan frequently. Once the clams open, remove from the heat. Remove the clams from their shells and place in a small bowl and cover. Discard any unopened clams. Reserve all liquid and strain to remove any sand or grit.

In a medium saucepan heat the olive oil and garlic over medium heat. Cook until the garlic becomes soft, stirring frequently so it does not brown. Add the white wine and bring to a boil to evaporate the alcohol. Add the salt, pepper, parsley, and clams. Cook just long enough so that the clams are warmed. Taste for salt and pepper.

Serve over pasta.

4 SERVINGS

RECOMMENDED PASTAS: Durum-wheat spaghetti or linguine, lemon or garlic-and-parsley fettuccine

APPROXIMATE NUTRITIONAL ANALYSIS PER SERVING OF SAUCE
205 calories, 7g protein, 3g carbohydrates, 2g complex carbohydrates, 17g fat, 18mg cholesterol, 566mg sodium, 208mg potassium

SALMON AND LEMON SAUCE

Smoked salmon is a great convenience food to have on hand. It's wonderful when served as an appetizer on lightly buttered toast points with chopped onion and capers, and it also adapts well when used as the main ingredient in spreads and even sauces.

Try serving this simple and quick-to-prepare smoked salmon sauce with Lemon Pasta or with Mint Pasta.

2 tablespoons unsalted butter
2 shallots, finely minced
4 ounces smoked salmon, sliced and cut into thin strips
1 teaspoon finely grated lemon rind
2 tablespoons freshly squeezed lemon juice

1 cup light cream
1 teaspoon small capers, rinsed under cold water and drained
1 pinch freshly ground black pepper

1 pound pasta, cooked al dente
2 tablespoons finely minced fresh parsley

In a medium-sized skillet heat the butter over low heat. Add the shallots and sauté, stirring frequently. When the shallots are transparent, add the smoked salmon, lemon rind, and lemon juice. Stir gently to mix. Add the cream, capers, and black pepper. Stir gently and simmer for 5 minutes. Remove from the heat and pour over pasta. Sprinkle with parsley.

4 SERVINGS

RECOMMENDED PASTAS: Egg, lemon, mint, or durum-wheat fettuccine

APPROXIMATE NUTRITIONAL ANALYSIS PER SERVING OF SAUCE

167 calories, 7g protein, 4g carbohydrates, 0g complex carbohydrates, 14g fat, 44mg cholesterol, 250mg sodium, 167mg potassium

BROCCOLI AND ONION SAUCE
(SUGO DI BROCCOLI)

This recipe is an adaptation of a dish prepared by Anna Amendolara Nurse, a special friend, cook, and instructor. While Anna's recipe calls for cauliflower, I have chosen to use broccoli. Nevertheless, be sure to serve the sauce with durum-wheat ziti or penne, or with orecchiette.

6 quarts water
1 large broccoli (2 to 2½ pounds), trimmed
   and cut into 2-inch florets
2 tablespoons salt
½ cup extra-virgin olive oil
2 medium yellow onions, finely chopped
1 pound pasta, cooked al dente

1 cup water reserved from cooking pasta
1 tablespoon finely chopped fresh parsley
Pinch crushed red pepper

Freshly grated Pecorino Romano cheese
   for serving

In a large covered pot bring the water to a boil. Add the broccoli and salt and cook for approximately 5 to 8 minutes or until just tender. Drain well. Place the broccoli in a large bowl. Cover to keep warm.

In a medium-sized saucepan heat the olive oil over high heat. Add the onions. Sauté over very low heat for approximately 15 to 20 minutes, or until the onions are a rich golden color. Stir frequently so the onions do not brown.

In a large serving bowl toss to mix the pasta with the broccoli, onions, reserved water, parsley, and red pepper. Taste for salt and pepper. Serve with grated Pecorino Romano cheese.

6 SERVINGS

RECOMMENDED PASTAS: Durum-wheat pasta such as penne or ziti; also, orecchiette

APPROXIMATE NUTRITIONAL ANALYSIS PER SERVING OF SAUCE
217 calories, 5g protein, 11g carbohydrates, 1g complex carbohydrates, 19g fat, 0mg cholesterol, 2180mg sodium, 599mg potassium

BROCCOLI DI RAPE AND SAUSAGE

(BROCCOLI DI RAPE E SALSICCE)

Broccoli di rape, a leafy green vegetable with scattered clusters of broccolilike buds, is available at most food stores and greengrocers. This somewhat strong-flavored green mellows in flavor when cooked and blends well with the addition of fragrant fennel sausages.

6 tablespoons extra-virgin olive oil
4 links sweet Italian sausage
4 cloves garlic, peeled and crushed
2 pounds of broccoli di rape or mustard
   greens, large, thick stems cut off and
   discarded, rinsed and well-drained

¼ teaspoon crushed red pepper
1 teaspoon salt
1 cup chicken stock

1 pound pasta, cooked al dente
Freshly grated Pecorino Romano cheese

In a large skillet with a cover heat 2 tablespoons of the olive oil. Add the sausages. Cook over medium heat. Turn to brown on all sides. Remove and pour off fat.

Add the remaining 4 tablespoons of olive oil. Add the garlic and sauté until golden. Add the broccoli di rape, crushed red pepper, and salt. Cover with the lid and steam over medium heat for 5 to 8 minutes, or until just cooked. Add the sausages and chicken stock. Bring to a boil. Remove from the heat. Taste for salt.

In a large serving bowl mix the pasta with the broccoli di rape and sausages. Serve with Pecorino Romano cheese.

4 SERVINGS

RECOMMENDED PASTAS: Durum-wheat pasta such as penne, ziti, or spaghetti; also, orecchiette

APPROXIMATE NUTRITIONAL ANALYSIS PER SERVING OF SAUCE

443 calories, 20g protein, 7g carbohydrates, 2g complex carbohydrates, 38g fat, 52mg cholesterol, 1381mg sodium, 723mg potassium

ROASTED VEGETABLE SAUCE
(SALSA ALLA NAPOLETANA CON VERDURE)

No other sauce better epitomizes the flavors of late summer than this one made from flavorful, sun-ripened vegetables. Many Mediterranean cuisines roast vegetables like ripe tomatoes, peppers, and eggplant and prepare them in hearty, delicious salads. The flavors of these vegetables blend well when mixed with a chunky pasta like ziti.

1 large eggplant
2 large red bell peppers
1 large green bell pepper
2 small zucchini
2 small yellow onions, unpeeled
6 medium ripe plum tomatoes
½ cup extra-virgin olive oil
2 tablespoons finely minced garlic
2 tablespoons balsamic or red wine
  vinegar

2 tablespoons finely minced fresh parsley
2 teaspoons salt
½ teaspoon freshly ground black pepper

1 pound pasta, cooked al dente
Freshly grated Parmesan cheese for
  serving

Prepare and light a barbecue grill or preheat the oven broiler. Wash and dry the vegetables. Prick the eggplant a few times with a fork. Place all the vegetables on the preheated barbecue grill or on a baking sheet under the broiler. Turn periodically so that the vegetables roast evenly. They are done when they are slightly charred on the outside and test soft when pricked with a fork. Remove from the heat as they are ready.

Put the roasted peppers in a paper bag and fold down the top. This will steam them and facilitate peeling. After 15 minutes, remove the peppers and peel off the charred skin. Discard the seeds and stems. Coarsely chop the peppers and put in a large bowl.

Split the eggplant in half. Remove the seeds. Scoop out the flesh and coarsely chop. Put in the bowl with the peppers.

Coarsely chop the zucchini and add to the bowl with the other vegetables.

Peel the tomatoes and onions. Coarsely chop and mix with the other vegetables.

In a small saucepan heat the olive oil and garlic over medium heat. Cook until the garlic becomes golden, stirring frequently so that it does not brown. Remove from the heat and pour over the prepared, chopped, roasted vegetables. Add the vinegar, parsley, salt, and pepper. Mix to combine. Let the flavors blend for at least 1 hour before serving. Taste for salt and pepper.

In a large serving bowl toss the drained pasta with the sauce. Serve either hot or at room temperature with Parmesan cheese.

4 SERVINGS

RECOMMENDED PASTAS: Durum-wheat pasta such as penne, ziti, or orecchiette

APPROXIMATE NUTRITIONAL ANALYSIS PER SERVING OF SAUCE

330 calories, 3g protein, 21g carbohydrates, 3g complex carbohydrates, 28g fat, 0mg cholesterol, 1084mg sodium, 747mg potassium

PRIMAVERA SAUCE

(SUGO DI VERDURE)

The creation of pasta primavera, a rich mélange of fresh vegetables, tomatoes, and cream served over pasta, is attributed to Sirio Maccioni, renowned restaurateur and owner of Le Cirque. The following is my version of this wonderful sauce.

1 pound broccoli, trimmed and cut into
  small florets and 1-inch pieces
2 small zucchini, cut into ½-inch cubes
8 ounces asparagus, trimmed and cut into
  1-inch pieces
4 tablespoons extra-virgin olive oil
1 large clove garlic, finely minced
5 large canned plum tomatoes, seeded
  and coarsely chopped
2 tablespoons finely chopped fresh basil
8 ounces mushrooms, thinly sliced

½ cup fresh or frozen peas
2 tablespoons finely chopped fresh
  parsley
1½ teaspoons salt
¼ teaspoon freshly ground black pepper
4 tablespoons unsalted butter
¾ cup light cream
½ cup freshly grated Parmesan cheese

1 pound pasta, cooked al dente

Steam the broccoli, zucchini, and asparagus until tender-crisp. Put in a large bowl and cover.

In a large skillet heat the olive oil and garlic over medium heat. When the garlic begins to sizzle, add the tomatoes. Cook for 2 minutes, stirring frequently. Add the basil and mushrooms. Sauté for 3 minutes. Add the peas, parsley, salt, and pepper. Cook for 2 minutes more. Remove from the skillet and add to the vegetables in the bowl.

Melt the butter in the same pan. Stir in the cream and Parmesan cheese. Stir constantly until smooth. Add the cooked pasta. Toss to coat. Stir in the vegetables. Heat just until hot.

4 SERVINGS

RECOMMENDED PASTAS: All types of egg pasta extruded through the fettuccine or linguine die; also, durum-wheat thin spaghetti or linguine, and tagliatelle or farfalle

APPROXIMATE NUTRITIONAL ANALYSIS PER SERVING OF SAUCE

369 calories, 15g protein, 20g carbohydrates, 3g complex carbohydrates, 28g fat, 58mg cholesterol, 1230mg sodium, 1059mg potassium

WILD MUSHROOM SAUCE
(SALSA DI FUNGHI)

Because of advances in domestic growing methods, wild mushrooms are now readily available year-round in most food stores and greengrocers'. This woodsy-flavored sauce goes well with a wide variety of pastas.

½ ounce dried porcini mushrooms (see Note)
1 cup boiling water
3 tablespoons extra-virgin olive oil
4 tablespoons unsalted butter
2 medium shallots, finely minced
1 pound assorted wild mushrooms, cleaned and sliced thick (choose from: cremini, shiitake, chanterelles, portobello, and oyster mushrooms)

2 tablespoons finely minced fresh parsley
1½ teaspoons salt
⅛ teaspoon freshly ground black pepper

1 pound pasta, cooked al dente
Freshly grated Parmesan cheese for serving

Soak the dried porcini in the boiling water for 20 minutes. With a slotted spoon remove the porcini from the water and chop into small pieces. Strain the soaking water to remove any dirt particles, and set aside.

In a large skillet heat the oil and butter over medium heat. Sauté the shallots over low heat for 2 to 3 minutes, or until soft. Add the sliced mushrooms and sauté over medium heat until they wilt and soften, about 5 to 8 minutes, stirring frequently. Add the chopped porcini and the reserved soaking liquid, parsley, salt, and pepper. Remove from the heat. Taste for salt and pepper.

Serve over pasta with grated Parmesan cheese.

4 SERVINGS

RECOMMENDED PASTAS: All types of egg pasta extruded through the fettuccine die; also, pappardelle, maltagliati, or farfalle

NOTE: Dried porcini mushrooms are available in most specialty-food stores or from mail-order catalogues.

APPROXIMATE NUTRITIONAL ANALYSIS PER SERVING OF SAUCE

238 calories, 3g protein, 10g carbohydrates, 4g complex carbohydrates, 22g fat, 31mg cholesterol, 808mg sodium, 521mg potassium

ZUCCHINI WITH GARLIC AND OLIVE OIL

(ZUCCHINI CON AGLIO E OLIO)

Sicilian cooking is relatively unknown when compared to the culinary renown of other regions of Italy. Since fresh vegetables abound in Sicily, there are endless pasta and vegetables dishes. Fried zucchini and pasta is a Sicilian favorite.

Vegetable oil for frying
1 pound zucchini, sliced into 1/16-inch-
   thick rounds
4 tablespoons extra-virgin olive oil
2 tablespoons finely minced garlic

1 pound pasta, cooked al dente
1/4 cup water reserved from cooking pasta
3 tablespoons finely minced parsley
Freshly grated Pecorino Romano cheese
   and ground black pepper for serving

In a large skillet heat 1/2 inch of vegetable oil over medium heat. Fry the zucchini slices in a single layer until golden brown, about 1 or 2 minutes. Turn over if necessary to fry on the other side. Drain on paper toweling.

In a small saucepan heat the olive oil and garlic over medium heat. Cook until the garlic becomes golden, about 2 to 3 minutes, stirring frequently so that it does not brown.

Remove from the heat and pour the garlic and oil over the pasta. Add the reserved water and toss with the fried zucchini and parsley.

Serve with Pecorino Romano cheese and black pepper.

4 SERVINGS

RECOMMENDED PASTAS: Durum-wheat spaghetti or linguine; also, lemon or mint pasta

APPROXIMATE NUTRITIONAL ANALYSIS PER SERVING OF SAUCE

143 calories, 2g protein, 5g carbohydrates, 1g complex carbohydrates, 14g fat, 0mg cholesterol, 6mg sodium, 314mg potassium

GARLIC AND OLIVE OIL SAUCE
(AGLIO E OLIO)

Made with the simplest of ingredients, spaghetti with garlic and oil is one of the very few pasta dishes eaten universally throughout Italy. This is especially remarkable when you take into account that every region and province has its own favorites particular to that area.

Make with the very finest extra-virgin olive oil available to you for an intense, fruity olive flavor. For best results, prepare the sauce while the pasta is cooking.

½ cup extra-virgin olive oil
2 tablespoons finely minced garlic
1 pound pasta, cooked al dente
⅓ cup water reserved from cooking pasta

2 tablespoons finely minced fresh parsley
Freshly ground black pepper, to taste
Freshly grated Pecorino Romano cheese
  for serving

In a small saucepan heat the olive oil and garlic over medium heat. Cook until the garlic becomes golden, stirring frequently so the garlic does not brown.

Remove from the heat and pour over the cooked, drained pasta. Add the reserved water, parsley, and black pepper. Toss to mix. Serve with grated Pecorino Romano cheese.

4 SERVINGS

RECOMMENDED PASTAS: Durum-wheat spaghetti or linguine

APPROXIMATE NUTRITIONAL ANALYSIS PER SERVING OF SAUCE
246 calories, 0g protein, 2g carbohydrates, 1g complex carbohydrates, 27g fat, 0mg cholesterol, 2mg sodium, 28mg potassium

BUTTER AND SAGE SAUCE
(BURRO ORO E SALVIA)

It's amazing how sometimes the simplest of ingredients can make the greatest impact. Made with only unsalted butter and fragrant fresh sage, the following recipe is well suited to a richly flavored pasta where the flavors are gently blended together.

6 tablespoons unsalted butter, cut into
  ½-inch pieces
8 whole fresh sage leaves

1 pound pasta, cooked al dente
Freshly grated Parmesan cheese for
  serving

In a small saucepan heat the butter over medium heat. Add the sage leaves when the butter stops foaming and just begins to assume a rich, golden color. Cook for 1 or 2 minutes, stirring continuously.

Remove from the heat and pour over the pasta. Sprinkle generously with Parmesan cheese.

4 SERVINGS

RECOMMENDED PASTAS: Potato gnocchi, tortelloni, or agnolotti; also egg, spinach, carrot, or whole-wheat fettuccine

APPROXIMATE NUTRITIONAL ANALYSIS PER SERVING OF SAUCE

153 calories, 1g protein, 0g carbohydrates, 0g complex carbohydrates, 17g fat, 47mg cholesterol, 2mg sodium, 7mg potassium

PESTO SAUCE
(PESTO)

The following is an interesting takeoff on the more familiar pesto sauce. Given to me by a Peruvian friend, this recipe is made in Peru using *queso fresco*, which is not unlike feta cheese.

2 medium cloves garlic
2 cups fresh basil leaves, packed
½ cup extra-virgin olive oil
½ cup (approximately 3 ounces) crumbled
   feta cheese
¼ cup chopped walnuts

1 pound pasta, cooked al dente
Freshly grated Parmesan cheese for
   serving

Put the garlic, basil leaves, and olive oil in a blender jar or food-processor bowl. Process until smooth. Add the feta cheese and walnuts and process just until the cheese is blended into the mixture. The sauce should have the same consistency as heavy cream. If too thick, add additional oil or water, a tablespoon at a time.

Serve over pasta with grated Parmesan cheese.

4 SERVINGS

RECOMMENDED PASTAS: All types of durum-wheat or egg pastas or potato gnocchi

APPROXIMATE NUTRITIONAL ANALYSIS PER SERVING OF SAUCE
376 calories, 6g protein, 4g carbohydrates, 1g complex carbohydrates, 38g fat, 27mg cholesterol, 344mg sodium, 161mg potassium

SUN-DRIED TOMATO AND PASTA SALAD

Drying tomatoes in the hot Mediterranean sun was one of the oldest methods used to preserve bumper crops of summer tomatoes. Readily available today in most food stores and from specialty-food catalogues, sun-dried tomatoes are sold either in their dried state or packed in olive oil.

1 pound pasta, cooked al dente, drained and rinsed under cold water
¾ cup sun-dried tomatoes packed in olive oil, drained, 2 tablespoons of oil reserved

2 tablespoons extra-virgin olive oil
2 cloves garlic, finely minced
18 large, fresh basil leaves
Salt and freshly ground black pepper to taste

Cut the sun-dried tomatoes into thin slivers. Add to the pasta in a large mixing bowl. Add the reserved oil, olive oil, garlic, and basil leaves. Season with salt and pepper.
   Serve at room temperature.

10 SERVINGS

RECOMMENDED PASTAS: Durum-wheat penne or ziti cut at 1-inch lengths

APPROXIMATE NUTRITIONAL ANALYSIS PER SERVING WITHOUT THE PASTA
61 calories, 1g protein, 4g carbohydrates, 0.5g complex carbohydrates, 5g fat, 0mg cholesterol, 45mg sodium, 273mg potassium

MOROCCAN CHARMOULA AND PASTA SALAD

Charmoula is a pungent Moroccan sauce traditionally served with fish. When combined with pasta and tuna, charmoula transforms these simplest of ingredients into a perfect meal for a light summer's dinner with a Mediterranean flair.

1 pound pasta, cooked al dente, drained
    and rinsed under cold water

CHARMOULA

½ cup extra-virgin olive oil
¼ cup freshly squeezed lemon juice
½ cup loosely packed fresh parsley leaves,
    coarsely chopped
½ cup loosely packed fresh cilantro
    leaves, coarsely chopped

3 cloves garlic, finely minced
1 teaspoon salt
½ teaspoon sweet paprika
½ teaspoon ground cumin
⅛ teaspoon cayenne pepper

Two 6⅛-ounce cans chunk light tuna
    packed in oil (preferably olive oil),
    drained
1 small red onion, halved and thinly
    sliced

1 cup cherry tomato halves
½ cup oil-cured black olives
Salt and freshly ground black pepper, to
    taste

Place the charmoula ingredients in a blender jar or food-processor bowl. Blend together with an on/off motion, just until thick. Do not overblend.

In a large salad bowl gently toss together the pasta, tuna, red onion, cherry tomatoes, black olives, and charmoula. Taste for salt and pepper.

Serve at room temperature.

10 SERVINGS

RECOMMENDED PASTAS: Durum-wheat, lemon, garlic and parsley, or mint pasta, cut into 1-inch-long tubular shapes such as penne or ziti

APPROXIMATE NUTRITIONAL ANALYSIS PER SERVING WITHOUT PASTA

172 calories, 10g protein, 2g carbohydrates, 0.3g complex carbohydrates, 14g fat, 6mg cholesterol, 338mg sodium, 119mg potassium

BAKED PASTA

SERVED AS FAR BACK as the times of the Romans, baked pastas are among the oldest types of pasta dishes. Today baked pasta dishes are extremely commonplace, which can be unfortunate if they are not made from the best ingredients available. Using fresh egg pasta from your pasta machine is a good beginning for outstanding results. Coupled with homemade sauce and quality cheeses, these dishes will make any day of the week seem special.

BAKED LASAGNE

It is interesting how we seem to take certain foods for granted. Lasagne has become almost commonplace, being right up there with spaghetti and meatballs. In Italy, however, it holds a special place of honor in the realm of pasta, since it is usually prepared and served only on very special occasions and holidays.

1 pound Lasagne noodles (page 66), cooked al dente, rinsed under cold water, drained, and placed individually on a clean kitchen towel until ready to use

5 cups Sunday Meat Sauce (page 102) (reserve meats for serving on the side or as a second course)
1½ pounds ricotta
1 pound mozzarella, coarsely shredded
½ cup freshly grated Parmesan cheese

Preheat the oven to 375° F. Cover the bottom of a 9-by-13-by-3-inch baking dish with a cup of the tomato sauce. Put a layer of noodles on the bottom of the baking dish, overlapping slightly. Spoon approximately a third of the ricotta on top of the lasagne. Sprinkle with a quarter of the mozzarella and then a quarter of the grated Parmesan cheese. Cover evenly with approximately 1 cup tomato sauce. Start again with the next layer, finishing up with a final layer of lasagne, tomato sauce, mozzarella cheese, and grated Parmesan cheese.

Put the lasagne in the preheated oven and bake for approximately 30 minutes, or until it is bubbling. Remove from the oven and let sit approximately 10 minutes before cutting.

8 SERVINGS

APPROXIMATE NUTRITIONAL ANALYSIS PER SERVING

760 calories, 45g protein, 46g carbohydrates, 35g complex carbohydrates, 44g fat, 283mg cholesterol, 1130mg sodium, 561mg potassium

BAKED MANICOTTI AND CANNELLONI

Manicotti and cannelloni are delicate shells of egg pasta. *Manicotti* ("muffs" in Italian, because of the shape the pasta takes when it is rolled) is stuffed with ricotta cheese. Cannelloni are filled with a flavorful meat-and-cheese filling.

18 Manicotti/Cannelloni shells (page 67), cooked al dente, rinsed under cold water, drained, and placed on a clean kitchen cloth until ready to use

3 cups Tomato Sauce (page 96), Tomato and Cream Sauce (page 97), Sunday Meat Sauce (page 102), or Bolognese Tomato and Meat Sauce (page 104)

MANICOTTI

FILLING

1½ cups ricotta
½ cup coarsely shredded mozzarella
4 tablespoons freshly grated Parmesan cheese

1 tablespoon finely chopped fresh parsley

½ cup freshly grated Parmesan cheese for sprinkling

Preheat the oven to 400° F. Spread 1 cup of tomato sauce on the bottom of a 9-by-13-by-1-inch nonreactive baking pan.

In a medium mixing bowl blend together the filling ingredients.

Place 2 to 3 tablespoons of the filling along the long edge of each manicotti shell, ½ inch from the ends. Roll up each shell jelly-roll fashion. Place with seam side down on the prepared baking dish. Cover with the remaining sauce and sprinkle with the Parmesan cheese. Bake for 15 to 20 minutes.

6 SERVINGS

APPROXIMATE NUTRITIONAL ANALYSIS PER SERVING WITHOUT SAUCE

64 calories, 34g protein, 55g carbohydrates, 45g complex carbohydrates, 28g fat, 242mg cholesterol, 693mg sodium, 463mg potassium

CANNELLONI

FILLING

2 tablespoons unsalted butter
2 tablespoons finely minced yellow onion
8 ounces ground lean beef
4 ounces ground lean veal
½ teaspoon salt
¼ teaspoon freshly ground nutmeg
1 tablespoon finely chopped fresh parsley

1 large egg, beaten
½ cup freshly grated Parmesan cheese
3 cups Tomato Sauce (page 96) or Tomato and Cream Sauce (page 97)

Freshly grated Parmesan cheese for sprinkling

In a large skillet heat the butter over medium heat. Add the onion. Sauté until the onion is transparent. Stir frequently so the onion does not brown. Add the ground beef and veal. Cook, stirring frequently, just until the meat loses its pink color.

Transfer the meat mixture to a blender jar or food-processor bowl. Add the remaining filling ingredients. Blend with an on/off motion just until smooth.

Preheat the oven to 375° F. Spread 1 cup tomato sauce on the bottom of a 9-by-13-by-1-inch nonreactive baking dish. Place 2 to 3 tablespoons of the filling along the long edge of each cannelloni shell, ½ inch from the ends. Roll up jelly-roll fashion. Place with the seam side down on the prepared baking dish. Cover with the remaining sauce and sprinkle with the Parmesan cheese. Bake for 20 to 25 minutes.

6 SERVINGS

APPROXIMATE NUTRITIONAL ANALYSIS PER SERVING WITHOUT SAUCE

605 calories, 32g protein, 54g carbohydrates, 45g complex carbohydrates, 28g fat, 282mg cholesterol, 868mg sodium, 573mg potassium

MANICOTTI AND CANNELLONI

1. *Place the filling along the long edge of each pasta shell ½ inch from the ends.*

2. *Roll up each shell jelly-roll fashion.*

3. *Place seam side down on the prepared baking dish.*

SOUPS

Soup is a wonderful comfort food. Enjoyed in all cultures, it is warm and nourishing, and full of all sorts of good things. My favorite soups almost always contain pasta or noodles.

Soups made from an herbal tomato base, with vegetables for substance, are low in fat and high in essential vitamins and minerals. Hearty soups like minestrone and Spanish seafood cazuela can be meals in themselves when served with some crusty bread and salad or fruit.

MINESTRONE

Minestrone is a thick Italian vegetable soup that simmers for over 2 hours, allowing the flavors of the different vegetables to blend together. Served with crusty bread and fresh fruit, minestrone is a meal in itself.

1½ cups Durum-Wheat Pasta (page 33), extruded through the penne or ziti die, cut at 1-inch lengths, cooked al dente

3 tablespoons extra-virgin olive oil
1 medium yellow onion, finely minced
3 cloves garlic, finely minced
1 tablespoon finely minced fresh parsley
1 tablespoon finely minced fresh basil
2 leaves fresh sage, torn into small pieces
1 cup canned plum tomatoes, seeded and coarsely chopped, with their juice
4 teaspoons salt
½ teaspoon freshly ground black pepper

1 cup finely diced carrots
1 cup finely diced celery
1 cup finely diced zucchini
1 cup finely diced potatoes
1 cup string beans, cut into ½-inch pieces
8 cups water
Rind from a 1-pound piece of Parmesan cheese, wiped clean (optional)
2 cups shredded cabbage
One 19-ounce can red kidney beans, well-drained
Freshly grated Parmesan cheese for serving

In a 6-quart pot heat the olive oil. Add the onion, garlic, and herbs. Sauté over medium heat for approximately 6 to 8 minutes. Stir frequently so the onion mixture does not brown.

Add the tomatoes, salt, and pepper. Mix well. Cook for approximately 6 minutes, stirring frequently. Add the vegetables, one at a time, mixing well before adding the next. Cook together, stirring frequently, for approximately 8 minutes.

Add the water and, if desired, the Parmesan cheese rind. Bring to a boil. Lower the heat. Cover and let simmer for 1½ hours, stirring periodically.

After 1½ hours, stir in the shredded cabbage. Cover and let simmer for 15 minutes. Stir in the drained kidney beans. Let simmer for 15 minutes longer. Remove from the heat. Let sit for 20 minutes. Taste for salt and pepper. Remove the cheese rind before serving.

Stir in the cooked pasta.
Serve with Parmesan cheese.

10 SERVINGS

APPROXIMATE NUTRITIONAL ANALYSIS PER SERVING, INCLUDING PASTA
315 calories, 11g protein, 56g carbohydrates, 44g complex carbohydrates, 5g fat, 0mg cholesterol, 1282 mg sodium, 635 mg potassium

CHICKEN SOUP WITH NOODLES

In the wintertime my mother used to make homemade chicken soup with noodles every Monday night. I remember how the windows in the kitchen used to steam up as the pot of soup slowly simmered. To this day there is still nothing as comforting for me as a steaming bowl of homemade chicken soup with noodles to take away the chill of winter.

8 ounces noodles such as Tagliatelle cut at 2-inch lengths (page 69), Maltagliati (page 80), Farfalle (page 81), cooked al dente
One 2½-to-3-pound chicken, with all visible fat removed
1½ cups finely diced carrots
1½ cups finely diced celery

2 sprigs celery leaves
1 medium whole yellow onion, peeled
1 large canned plum tomato, seeded and coarsely chopped
3 teaspoons salt
8 black peppercorns
Freshly grated Pecorino Romano cheese or snipped fresh dill for serving

Place the chicken in a 6-quart pot. Fill with cold water up to 1 inch from the top of the pot. Bring to a boil. Remove, with a slotted spoon, any foam or impurities that float to the top.

When no more foam appears, add the vegetables, salt, and peppercorns. Stir once to mix. Do not stir again or the soup will be cloudy. Lower the heat to a simmer. Let the soup reduce by one-third (approximately 1½ hours).

Remove the chicken from the soup. Discard the skin and bone the chicken. Shred the meat into small pieces. Discard the onion and celery leaves. Spoon off any excess fat floating on top of the soup. Add the shredded chicken to the soup, and taste for salt.

After cooking the noodles, return to the pot and add some chicken broth so the noodles will not dry out. Ladle the desired amount of noodles into individual soup bowls. Fill with soup.

Serve with Pecorino Romano cheese or fresh dill.

8 SERVINGS

APPROXIMATE NUTRITIONAL ANALYSIS PER SERVING

328 calories, 26g protein, 40g carbohydrates, 34g complex carbohydrates, 6g fat, 154mg cholesterol, 1131mg sodium, 431mg potassium

PASTA AND BEANS
(PASTA E FAGIOLI)

While dried beans are an age-old sustenance, they have recently become increasingly popular and dishes such as *pasta e fagioli* can even be found on the menus of four-star restaurants.

1 pound Durum-Wheat Pasta (page 33), extruded through the penne or ziti die and cut at 1-inch lengths; or Orecchiette (page 40), cooked al dente and drained
3 tablespoons extra-virgin olive oil, plus extra for serving
1 slice pancetta or unsmoked bacon, coarsely chopped
1 small yellow onion, finely chopped
1 clove garlic, peeled and crushed
2 leaves fresh sage, minced, or ½ teaspoon dried

1 small canned plum tomato, seeded and coarsely chopped
1 small carrot, diced into small cubes
1 stalk celery, diced into small cubes
1½ teaspoons salt
¼ teaspoon freshly ground black pepper
2 cups cooked cannellini or white kidney beans, drained
2 cups water reserved from cooking beans
4 cups water
Freshly grated Parmesan cheese for serving

In a medium-sized saucepan heat the 3 tablespoons olive oil over high heat. Add the pancetta, onion, garlic, and sage. Sauté over medium heat for 2 to 3 minutes or until the onion is transparent. Stir frequently so the onion does not brown. Add the tomato and sauté for 1 minute, stirring continuously. Add the carrot and celery and cook for 2 minutes more. Add the salt and black pepper and then the beans and the 6 cups water. Stir well. Cover and let simmer for 45 minutes, stirring occasionally.

Remove from the heat and add the cooked pasta. Stir well to blend. Drizzle lightly with extra-virgin olive oil and serve with Parmesan cheese.

4 SERVINGS

APPROXIMATE NUTRITIONAL ANALYSIS PER SERVING, INCLUDING PASTA
693 calories, 26g protein, 118g carbohydrates, 86g complex carbohydrates, 13g fat, 1mg cholesterol, 882mg sodium, 901mg potassium

SEAFOOD STEW WITH NOODLES
(CAZUELA MARINERA DE FIDEOS)

A *cazuela* is a popular earthenware skillet used throughout Spain. Renowned for its heat-retaining properties, it can be purchased at most housewares stores and from mail-order catalogues.

While Spainards are not large consumers of pasta and noodles, almost every Spanish cook has his or her own favorite version of *cazuela marinera de fideos*, a rich seafood stew.

8 ounces Durum-Wheat Pasta (page 33), extruded through the thin spaghetti die and cut into 3-inch lengths

1 pound small raw shrimp
6 cups water
2 teaspoons salt
1 large bay leaf
4 tablespoons extra-virgin olive oil
1 medium yellow onion, finely chopped
2 cloves garlic, finely minced

1 medium green bell pepper, finely chopped
2 large canned plum tomatoes, seeded and coarsely chopped
1 teaspoon sweet paprika
¼ teaspoon freshly ground black pepper
1 pound monkfish, cleaned and cut into large chunks
1 dozen littleneck clams, scrubbed and soaked for 1 hour in salted water
1 teaspoon finely minced fresh parsley

Peel and devein the shrimp, reserving the shells and tails. In a medium-sized saucepan bring the water to a boil. Add the shrimp shells and tails, salt, and bay leaf. Cover and let simmer for 15 minutes. Strain the broth and discard the shells and tails.

In a large clay cazuela or skillet heat the olive oil. Add the onion, garlic, and green pepper. Sauté over medium heat for 6 to 8 minutes, or until soft yet not browned. Add the tomatoes and sauté for 2 to 3 minutes, stirring frequently. Stir in the paprika and black pepper. Add the monkfish, clams, and 4 cups of the reserved broth. Bring to a simmer and let cook for 10 minutes. Add the spaghetti. Let cook for 3 minutes, then add the shrimp. Cook until the shrimp turn pink.

Remove from the heat and sprinkle with parsley. Taste for salt and pepper.

4 SERVINGS

NOTE: Although the cazuela should not be soupy, some liquid should remain when served. If the broth appears to be evaporating too quickly, lower the heat and add some of the reserved broth, a little at a time, so that the fish and noodles have enough liquid to cook in. Discard any clams that did not open when cooked.

APPROXIMATE NUTRITIONAL ANALYSIS PER SERVING

833 calories, 65g protein, 96g carbohydrates, 87g complex carbohydrates, 10g fat, 266mg cholesterol, 1424mg sodium, 1249mg potassium

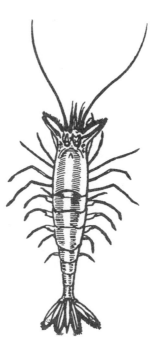

PASTA AND PEAS
(PASTA E PISELLI)

While I was growing up, meat was never eaten in our home on Friday. On Friday nights my mother would usually prepare old family favorites like pasta and peas or pasta and beans (preceding recipe). Simple yet nourishing, these are the comfort foods that I always remember.

1 pound Durum-Wheat Pasta (page 33), extruded through the penne or ziti die, cut at 1-inch lengths; or Orecchiette (page 40), cooked al dente and drained

3 tablespoons extra-virgin olive oil
1 medium yellow onion, finely chopped
5 large canned plum tomatoes, seeded and coarsely chopped, with their juice

2 sprigs fresh basil
1 teaspoon salt
½ teaspoon freshly ground black pepper
3 cups cooked fresh or frozen peas
1¼ cups water reserved from cooking pasta
Freshly grated Parmesan cheese for serving

In a medium-sized saucepan heat the olive oil over high heat. Add the onion and sauté over medium heat for 5 minutes, or until the onion is transparent and lightly golden. Stir frequently so it does not brown.

Add the tomatoes, basil, salt, and pepper. Bring to a boil. Lower the heat and simmer, uncovered, for 15 minutes, stirring periodically. Add the peas, pasta, and reserved water. Toss to mix. Taste for salt and pepper.

Serve with grated Parmesan cheese.

4 SERVINGS

APPROXIMATE NUTRITIONAL ANALYSIS PER SERVING, INCLUDING PASTA
661 calories, 23g protein, 114g carbohydrates, 92g complex carbohydrates, 12g fat, 0mg cholesterol, 640mg sodium, 727mg potassium

PASTA AND CAULIFLOWER
(PASTA E CAVOLFIORE)

Cauliflower is indeed a large flower made up of many tiny buds. This very simple-to-make soup, made from fresh cauliflower and a garlicky tomato-base broth, is sure to become a family favorite.

1 pound Durum-Wheat Pasta (page 33),
   extruded through the penne or ziti die,
   cooked al dente and drained

6 quarts water
1 large cauliflower (2½ to 3 pounds),
   trimmed and cut into 2-inch florets

2 tablespoons salt
1 cup Marinara Sauce (page 99)
Freshly grated black pepper, to taste
Freshly grated Pecorino Romano cheese
   for serving

In a large pot bring the water to a boil. Add the cauliflower and salt. Cook for 8 to 10 minutes or until tender. Drain, reserving 12 cups of water.

Return the reserved cauliflower water to the pot. Add the marinara sauce. Bring to a boil. Add the cooked cauliflower and pasta to heat through. Taste for salt and pepper.

Serve with grated Pecorino Romano cheese.

6 SERVINGS

APPROXIMATE NUTRITIONAL ANALYSIS PER SERVING
348 calories, 14g protein, 69g carbohydrates, 57g complex carbohydrates, 2g fat, 0mg cholesterol, 2164mg sodium, 451mg potassium

WON TON SOUP

Made from rich chicken stock, pieces of gingerroot, and scallions, this soup is easily distinguishable from all other chicken soups.

48 Won Tons (page 154)

2½ to 3 pounds chicken bones with meat, including backs, wings, and necks, with all fat and skin removed

4 pieces fresh gingerroot, sliced into ¼-inch pieces
2 large scallions, halved
Salt, to taste

Place the chicken bones in a 6-quart stockpot. Fill with cold water up to 1 inch from the top of the pot. Bring to a boil. With a slotted spoon remove any foam or impurities that float to the top.

Flatten the ginger and the scallions with the side of a chef's knife or cleaver to release their flavors. Once no more foam appears on top of the broth, add the ginger and scallions. Lower the heat to a simmer. Let the stock reduce by half (approximately 2 hours). So that the stock does not become cloudy, do not stir while cooking.

Once the stock is cooled, pour it through a fine mesh strainer. Refrigerate and skim off any fat.

When ready to use the stock, reheat in a 6-quart stockpot. Bring to a rolling boil. Taste for salt. Lower the heat to a simmer. Add uncooked won tons, one at a time. Let cook for 5 minutes or until the won ton filling loses its pink color.

6 SERVINGS

APPROXIMATE NUTRITION ANALYSIS PER SERVING

670 calories, 44g protein, 68g carbohydrates, 63g complex carbohydrates, 23g fat, 157mg cholesterol, 3233mg sodium, 949mg potassium

JAPANESE SOBA IN BROTH
(KAKE-SOBA)

Noodles in broth is the Japanese equivalent of fast food. Noodle shops are scattered throughout Japan and provide busy office workers with a quick midday respite from work.

1 pound fresh Japanese Buckwheat
   Noodles (page 91)

BROTH

4¼ cups water
1 ounce *konbu* (dried kelp—see Note)
1 ounce *hana-katsuo* (dried bonito flakes—see Note)

1 teaspoon salt
3 tablespoons soy sauce
1 tablespoon sugar

1 tablespoon *mirin* (sweet rice wine—see Note)
4 ounces small raw shrimp, peeled and deveined
4 ounces shiitake mushrooms, thinly sliced
4 tablespoons finely sliced scallions, white and green parts

In a medium-sized saucepan heat 4 cups of the water and the konbu. Remove from the heat once the water begins to boil. Remove the konbu and discard. Add the remaining ¼ cup of water and the hana-katsuo. Return to the heat. Once the water begins to boil, remove from the heat. Let steep until the bonito flakes settle to the bottom of the pot. Strain through a very fine tea strainer.

Wash the pot and add the broth, salt, soy sauce, sugar, and mirin. Stir well. Bring to a simmer over low heat. Add the noodles and cook for 4 or 5 minutes, or until al dente. Add the shrimp, mushrooms, and scallions. Simmer until the shrimp just turn pink. Serve in bowls.

4 SERVINGS

NOTE: Japanese ingredients are available in most Asian food stores or from mail-order catalogues.

APPROXIMATE NUTRITIONAL ANALYSIS PER SERVING, INCLUDING SOBA

329 calories, 15g protein, 64g carbohydrates, 51g complex carbohydrates, 2g fat, 55mg cholesterol, 1398mg sodium, 297mg potassium

ASIAN NOODLES, DUMPLINGS, AND SAUCES

SOME OF MY FONDEST dining memories while traveling in Asia are not from fancy restaurants, but from the exotic noodle shops and food stands that abound in the busy cities.

Fragrant with pieces of meat, seafood, and vegetables, Asian noodle dishes are a wonderfully balanced mixture of complex carbohydrates and protein. They can be light enough to be eaten as a snack or substantial enough to be a complete meal. Fortunately for us, Asian ingredients are readily available in most supermarkets, enabling us to enjoy these easy-to-prepare dishes at home.

LO MEIN

In China, as in most Asian countries, noodle shops and outdoor stands provide quick nourishment to the hungry. Lo mein, a universal favorite, is usually made with whatever meat, seafood, or vegetables may be on hand.

1 pound Chinese Egg Noodles (page 87),
    extruded through the spaghetti die,
    cooked al dente, drained, and rinsed
    under cold water

MARINADE

1 tablespoon white wine or dry sherry
1 tablespoon soy sauce
1 tablespoon cornstarch

4 ounces lean pork fillet or chicken breast,
    cut into thin matchstick strips

SAUCE

1 tablespoon soy sauce

½ cup chicken broth

3 tablespoons vegetable oil
2 large scallions, white and green parts,
    cut into thin matchstick strips
4 ounces snow peas, cut into thin
    matchstick strips

4 ounces mushrooms, cut into quarters
1 small carrot, cut into thin matchstick
    strips

In a medium-sized bowl mix together the marinade ingredients. Add the meat and stir to cover. Let sit for 30 minutes. Drain well. Discard the marinade.

In a small bowl mix together the sauce ingredients. Set aside.

In a wok or large skillet heat the vegetable oil over high heat. When the oil begins to smoke, add the marinated meat. Stir-fry until just cooked. Push to one side and add the vegetables. Stir-fry for 2 to 3 minutes, stirring constantly. Mix with the meat. Pour in the sauce. When the sauce begins to bubble, add the noodles. Toss lightly to mix together. Let cook until the noodles are hot.

Remove from the pan and serve.

APPROXIMATE NUTRITIONAL ANALYSIS PER SERVING, INCLUDING NOODLES

640 calories, 27g protein, 81g carbohydrates, 71g complex carbohydrates, 22g fat, 226mg cholesterol, 1101mg sodium, 553mg potassium

Cantonese Rice Noodles with Beef

(Kan Ch'ao Niu Ho)

This dish is an excellent example of how the Chinese take a small amount of meat, mix it with noodles and vegetables, and come up with a complete, well-balanced meal.

1 pound Rice Noodles (page 89), extruded
   through the angel-hair or thin spaghetti
   die, cooked al dente, drained, and
   rinsed under cold water

MARINADE

½ teaspoon salt
2 teaspoons soy sauce
1 tablespoon cornstarch
2 tablespoons water

1 tablespoon vegetable oil

8 ounces beef fillet, trimmed of all fat,
   thinly sliced and cut into thin strips

SAUCE

1 teaspoon sugar

3 tablespoons vegetable oil
1½ teaspoons finely minced fresh
   gingerroot

4 tablespoons soy sauce

2 large scallions, white and green parts,
   thinly sliced
¼ teaspoon salt
4 ounces snow peas

In a medium-sized bowl mix together the marinade ingredients. Add the beef and stir to cover. Let sit for 30 minutes.

In a small bowl, mix together the sauce ingredients. Set aside.

In a wok or large skillet heat 2 tablespoons of the vegetable oil over high heat. When the oil begins to smoke, add the ginger and scallions. Stirring constantly, cook for 30 seconds. Add the marinated beef and marinade. Stir-fry until the beef is just cooked and no longer pink in color. Remove the wok from the heat. Place the beef in a plate.

Heat the remaining tablespoon of oil in the wok. Add the salt. When the oil begins to smoke, add the snow peas. Stir-fry for approximately 1 minute. Add the cooked beef and rice noodles. Mix well. Pour in the sauce and mix thoroughly. Cook for 1 or 2 minutes or until the noodles are hot, stirring constantly.

Remove the wok from the heat and serve.

4 SERVINGS

APPROXIMATE NUTRITIONAL ANALYSIS PER SERVING, INCLUDING NOODLES

658 calories, 27g protein, 89g carbohydrates, 42g complex carbohydrates, 21g fat, 48mg cholesterol, 1639mg sodium, 458mg potassium

PAN-FRIED NOODLES WITH CHICKEN
(SAN SSU CH'AO MEIN)

This dish from Shanghai provides a wonderful departure from the more conventional stir-fried noodle dishes that most of us are familiar with. The precooked noodles are fried like a golden, crisp pancake, which is then covered with a chicken-and-vegetable stir-fry, fragrant with ginger and garlic.

8 ounces Chinese Egg Noodles (page 87), extruded through the thin spaghetti die, cooked al dente, drained, and rinsed under cold water

MARINADE

1 teaspoon sesame oil
1 teaspoon soy sauce
1 tablespoon white wine or dry sherry
1 teaspoon sugar

½ teaspoon cornstarch

8 ounces boneless chicken breasts, thinly sliced and cut into thin strips

SAUCE

1 teaspoon sesame oil
1 teaspoon white wine or dry sherry
2 teaspoons soy sauce
1 cup chicken broth

1 teaspoon sugar
½ teaspoon salt
¾ teaspoon cornstarch

5 tablespoons vegetable oil
1½ teaspoons finely minced fresh gingerroot
1 clove garlic, minced
1 small carrot thinly sliced diagonally, blanched

3 stalks broccoli, trunks only, thinly sliced, blanched
4 ounces white mushrooms, cut into quarters
4 ounces snow peas
2 large scallions, white and green parts, thinly sliced

In a medium-sized bowl mix together the marinade ingredients. Add the chicken and stir to cover. Let sit for 30 minutes.

In a small bowl mix together the sauce ingredients. Set aside.

Place the drained noodles in a 10-inch nonstick skillet. Let set for 15 minutes. Invert the noodles onto a dinner plate.

In a large skillet heat 2 tablespoons of the vegetable oil over medium heat. Carefully slide the noodles into the skillet. Let the noodles cook until golden brown. Invert onto a dinner plate. Slide the noodle pancake, uncooked side down, into the skillet. Cook until golden brown. Remove from the pan and place on a serving platter. Cover to keep warm.

In a wok or large skillet heat 1½ tablespoons of the vegetable oil over high heat. When the oil begins to smoke, add the ginger and garlic. Stirring constantly, cook for 30 seconds. Add the marinated chicken and marinade. Stir-fry just until the chicken is cooked. Remove the wok from the heat. Place the chicken on a plate.

Heat the remaining 1½ tablespoons of vegetable oil in the wok. When the oil begins to smoke, add the vegetables. Stir-fry for approximately 5 minutes. Add the cooked chicken. Mix well. Push the mixture to the sides to form a well in the center of the pan. Pour in the sauce. When the sauce begins to bubble, stir to combine with the chicken-and-vegetable mixture. Cook just until the sauce coats the mixture.

Remove the pan from the heat and pour over the pan-fried noodle pancake.

4 SERVINGS

APPROXIMATE NUTRITIONAL ANALYSIS PER SERVING, INCLUDING NOODLES
684 calories, 31g protein, 83g carbohydrates, 70g complex carbohydrates, 25g fat, 160mg cholesterol, 1343mg sodium, 656mg potassium

COLD SESAME NOODLES AND CHICKEN

(MA JIANG BAN MIAN)

Cold sesame noodles are a popular summer dish in China. The nutty flavor of the sesame paste appeals to Westerners, making this a perennial favorite in most restaurants.

1 pound Chinese Egg Noodles (page 87),
   extruded through the thin spaghetti
   die, cooked al dente, drained, and
   rinsed under cold water

SAUCE

3 tablespoons sesame paste (see Note) or
   creamy, all-natural peanut butter

1 teaspoon sugar
1 tablespoon sesame oil

1 tablespoon vegetable oil
2 tablespoons soy sauce
2 tablespoons chicken stock, reserved
   from poaching chicken

3 large scallions, white and green parts,
   thinly sliced
4 ounces poached chicken breast, cut into
   thin matchstick strips (strain and
   reserve cooking liquid)

In a medium-sized bowl blend together the sauce ingredients. Reserve 2 tablespoons of the sauce. Toss the cooked noodles with the remaining sauce. If too dry, add a couple of tablespoons of chicken stock.

Place the tossed noodles on a serving platter. Sprinkle with the scallions. Mound the cooked chicken on top, in the center. Drizzle the reserved sauce on top of the chicken.

4 SERVINGS

NOTE: Sesame paste, which is also called *tahini*, is available in some supermarkets and specialty-food stores.

APPROXIMATE NUTRITIONAL ANALYSIS PER SERVING, INCLUDING NOODLES

599 calories, 26g protein, 77g carbohydrates, 69g complex carbohydrates, 20g fat, 210mg cholesterol, 1074mg sodium, 362mg potassium

DIM SUM

Dim sum are small Chinese snacks that are stuffed with a wide variety of fillings. The ones that follow are dumplings made from won ton skins.

Dim sum can either be served as appetizers or as a main course. Various dipping sauces are included for your eating pleasure.

WON TONS
(YUN TUN)

You will be quite surprised to taste how delicious won tons are when they are home-made. The thin noodle covering melts in your mouth to reveal a moist, flavorful center of meat and seasonings.

Use these won tons in soup (page 142) or steam them to be eaten as dim sum.

48 Won Ton Skins (page 85), 3 inches square

FILLING

2 tablespoons water
2 teaspoons white wine or dry sherry
½ teaspoon sesame oil
1 tablespoon cornstarch

1 teaspoon salt
1 pound lean ground pork
1 tablespoon thinly sliced green scallion
 tops

In a medium-sized bowl stir together the water, wine, sesame oil, cornstarch, and salt. Mix with the ground pork and scallion tops until smooth.

Place a scant teaspoon of filling in the center of a won ton skin. Wet your index finger in a small bowl of water and moisten the edges. Fold the won ton in half diagonally to form a triangle and gently pinch the edges together to seal. Moisten the two opposite points of the triangle. Bring the points together and pinch to join. Fold down. Lightly sprinkle a clean kitchen cloth with cornstarch and place the prepared won tons on the cloth until ready to use. Keep covered with another clean cloth so the won tons do not dry out.

To cook in broth, add to slowly simmering stock and cook for approximately 15 minutes, or until the filling just loses its pink color.

To steam the won tons, use a Chinese bamboo steamer placed over a pan or wok of boiling water, or use a covered metal steamer that has been lightly oiled. Steam the won tons for 5 to 10 minutes, or until the filling loses its pink color.

Serve as an appetizer or as a light supper with other dim sum.

48 SERVINGS

APPROXIMATE NUTRITIONAL ANALYSIS PER WON TON

70 calories each, 4g protein, 8g carbohydrates, 7g complex carbohydrates, 2g fat, 140mg sodium, 47mg potassium

WON TONS

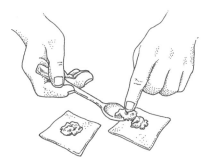

1. Place the filling in the center of each square of dough.

2. Lightly dampen the edges with water and fold in half diagonally to form a triangle. Squeeze the edges together to seal well.

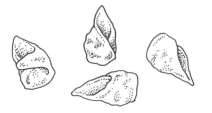

3. Bring the two bottom points of the triangle together and pinch to join.

POT STICKERS
(KWO TIEH)

Pot stickers are another of the numerous versions of dim sum. These small meat-filled dumplings are steamed and then quickly browned on one side. Once you get the hang of making these, you will be surprised how quick and easy they are to prepare.

50 Won Ton Skins (page 85), 3 inches in
    diameter, using biscuit cutter

FILLING

1 teaspoon sugar
1 teaspoon salt
1½ tablespoons cornstarch
1½ tablespoons soy sauce
1 tablespoon white wine or dry sherry
1 tablespoon water
1 teaspoon sesame oil
1 pound lean ground pork

2 tablespoons thinly sliced green scallion
    tops
4 ounces canned bamboo shoots, finely
    minced, drained, and rinsed under cold
    water

1 to 2 tablespoons vegetable oil for
    browning dumplings

In a medium-sized bowl stir together the sugar, salt, cornstarch, soy sauce, wine, water, and sesame oil. Mix with the ground pork, scallion tops, and bamboo shoots until smooth.

Place a scant teaspoon of filling in the center of a won ton skin. Wet your index finger in a small bowl of water and moisten the edges. Fold the dumpling in half to form a half-moon and crimp the edges to seal. Lightly sprinkle a clean kitchen cloth with cornstarch and place the prepared dumplings on the cloth, until ready to use. Keep covered with another clean cloth so the dumplings do not dry out. Pot stickers can either be cooked immediately or stored for later use (page 23).

To steam the dumplings, use a Chinese bamboo steamer placed over a pan or wok of boiling water, or use a lightly oiled, covered metal steamer. Steam the dumplings for 5 to 10 minutes, or until the filling loses its pink color.

In a large nonstick skillet heat the oil until it begins to smoke. Add the steamed dumplings, flat side up, and brown while shaking the skillet constantly. Remove the dumplings from the pan when they are golden brown.

POT STICKERS

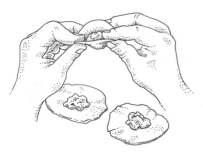 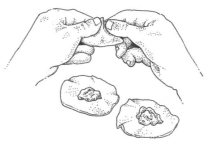

1. *Place the filling in the center of each circle of dough.*

2. *Lightly dampen the edges with water. Fold the circle of dough in half.*

3. *Crimp the edges by forming small pleats along the curved edges of the pot sticker.*

Serve as an appetizer or as a light supper with other dim sum.

50 SERVINGS

APPROXIMATE NUTRITIONAL ANALYSIS PER POT STICKER

76 calories each, 4g protein, 8g carbohydrates, 7g complex carbohydrates, 3g fat, 19mg cholesterol, 169mg sodium, 73mg potassium

SHRIMP BEGGAR'S PURSES

(SZU HSI CHIAO)

These have to be the most festive-looking of all dim sum. The puréed filling is light and flavorful, and when the shrimp are steamed they turn a pretty pink.

The tails of the shrimp can be used as a built-in utensil, making these the ultimate in finger food!

30 Won Ton Skins (page 85), 3 inches in
    diameter, using biscuit cutter

FILLING

1 pound small raw shrimp, peeled and
    deveined, tails left on half the shrimp
1 teaspoon thinly sliced scallion, white
    part only
2 cloves garlic, finely minced
1 teaspoon white wine or dry sherry

1 teaspoon soy sauce
¾ teaspoon salt
1 large egg white
1 tablespoon cornstarch
¾ cup fresh or frozen peas

Rinse the shrimp under cold water and drain well. In a blender or food processor, blend half the shrimp to a fine paste or mince fine with a knife. In a medium-sized bowl, blend together the remaining filling ingredients. Add the shrimp paste and blend well.

Place ½ teaspoon of shrimp filling in the center of each dumpling skin. Spread slightly. Place a whole shrimp on the top of the filling with the tail pointing up. Wet your index finger in a small bowl of water and moisten the edges of the dumpling skin. Carefully pull the edge of the dumpling up toward the center, pinching to seal around the shrimp (the tail will be sticking up and out). Sprinkle a clean kitchen cloth with cornstarch and place the prepared dumplings on the cloth until ready to use. Keep covered with another clean cloth so the dumplings do not dry out. Beggar's purses can either be cooked at this point or stored for later use (page 23).

To steam the dumplings, use a Chinese bamboo steamer placed over a pan or wok of boiling water, or use a covered metal steamer that has been lightly oiled. Steam the dumplings for 5 to 10 minutes, or until the filling and shrimp have turned pink.

Serve as an appetizer or as a light supper with other dim sum.

30 SERVINGS

BEGGAR'S PURSES

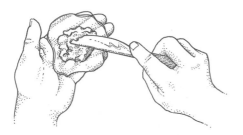

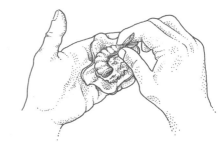

1. Place the filling in the center of each circle of dough. Spread slightly.

2. Place a shrimp on top of the filling with the tail pointing up.

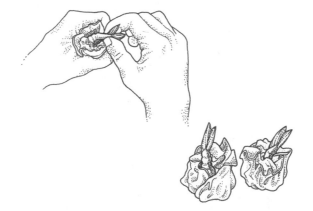

3. Lightly dampen the edges of the dumpling skin. Carefully pull up the dumpling skin, pinching to seal around the shrimp tail.

APPROXIMATE NUTRITION ANALYSIS PER BEGGAR'S PURSE

44 calories, 4g protein, 5g carbohydrates, 5g complex carbohydrates, 1g fat, 38mg cholesterol, 177mg sodium, 42mg potassium

Dim Sum Dipping Sauces

Prepare and serve any of these sauces with dim sum.

GINGER SAUCE

1 teaspoon grated gingerroot
1 large scallion, white and green parts,
   thinly sliced
1½ teaspoons sugar

3 tablespoons soy sauce
2 tablespoons water
1 teaspoon sesame oil

In a small bowl mix all the ingredients to blend. Makes about ⅓ cup.

APPROXIMATE NUTRITIONAL ANALYSIS PER TEASPOON

4 calories, 0g protein, 1g carbohydrates, 0g complex carbohydrates, 0g fat, 0mg cholesterol, 131mg sodium, 6mg potassium

HONEY MUSTARD SAUCE

1 clove garlic, finely minced
½ teaspoon mustard powder
2 tablespoons honey

4 tablespoons soy sauce
1 tablespoon water

In a small bowl mix all the ingredients to blend. Makes approximately ½ cup.

APPROXIMATE NUTRITIONAL ANALYSIS PER TEASPOON

7 calories, 0g protein, 2g carbohydrates, 0g complex carbohydrates, 0g fat, 0mg cholesterol, 143mg sodium, 7mg potassium

Chili Sauce

½ teaspoon crushed red pepper
½ teaspoon sugar
1 large scallion, white and green parts,
  thinly sliced

4 tablespoons soy sauce
1 tablespoon water
2 teaspoons sesame oil

In a small bowl mix all the ingredients to blend. Makes approximately ⅓ cup.

Approximate nutritional analysis per teaspoon

6 calories, 0g protein, 0g carbohydrates, 0g complex carbohydrates, 0g fat, 0mg cholesterol, 174mg sodium, 8mg potassium

CURRIED SINGAPORE RICE NOODLES

(XING ZHOU CHAO MI)

Singapore is the melting pot of Asia. Comprising a Chinese majority, with Malay and Indian minorities, Singapore boasts a cuisine that clearly reflects the influences these cultures have played over the course of time.

1 pound Rice Noodles (page 89), extruded through the angel-hair or thin spaghetti die, cooked al dente, drained, and rinsed under cold water

3 tablespoons vegetable oil
4 large scallions, white and green parts, thinly sliced

12 ounces Chinese roast pork, cut into thin slices (see Note)
4 ounces small raw shrimp, peeled and deveined
1 tablespoon soy sauce
1 small yellow onion, finely chopped
1½ tablespoons curry powder
¼ cup chicken broth

In a wok or large skillet heat 1 tablespoon of the oil over high heat. When the oil begins to smoke, add the scallions. Stirring constantly, cook for 30 seconds. Add the roast pork and shrimp. Stir-fry just until the shrimp turn pink, 1 to 2 minutes. Add the soy sauce. Stir to cover. Place the cooked pork and shrimp in a bowl and set aside.

Wipe out the pan with a paper towel and return it to the heat. Heat the remaining 2 tablespoons of oil over high heat. When the oil begins to smoke, add the onion and stir-fry for 1 minute. Add the curry powder and stir-fry for 1 minute longer. Add the broth and bring to a boil. Add the noodles and stir to cover. Add the pork and shrimp and cook together for 1 minute, tossing frequently.

4 SERVINGS

NOTE: Either purchase Chinese roast pork from a local Chinese restaurant or prepare beforehand as in following recipe:

(continued)

ROAST PORK

1 teaspoon salt
3 tablespoons sugar
1½ tablespoons white wine or sherry
1½ tablespoons soy sauce

1½ tablespoons hoisin sauce
1 pork tenderloin (approximately
   1 pound), trimmed of all fat

In a large glass or ceramic bowl or deep dish blend the salt, sugar, wine, soy, and hoisin sauces. Marinate the meat overnight, turning periodically.

Preheat the oven to 425° F. Remove the meat from the marinade and place on a rack in a small roasting pan. Cook for 20 to 25 minutes, or until the meat appears crisp on the outside and has lost its pink color when cut. Let cool and slice very thin.

8 SERVINGS

APPROXIMATE NUTRITIONAL INFORMATION PER SERVING

671 calories, 34g protein, 95g carbohydrates, 40g complex carbohydrates, 16g fat, 67mg cholesterol, 1020mg sodium, 584mg potassium

THAI RICE NOODLES WITH BROCCOLI

(RAD NA GWAYTIO)

Thai stir-fried rice noodles with broccoli and meat is one of many popular lunch dishes found in many of the "fast food" outdoor restaurants in Bangkok. It is simple to make and can also be served as a light entrée for dinner.

1 pound Rice Noodles (page 89), extruded
   through the linguine die, cooked al
   dente, drained, and rinsed under cold
   water

SAUCE

2 tablespoons oyster sauce (see Note)
1½ tablespoons fish sauce (see Note)

1 teaspoon cornstarch
1 cup chicken stock

3 tablespoons vegetable oil
1½ tablespoons finely minced garlic
8 ounces boneless chicken breast, thinly
   sliced and cut into thin strips

1 tablespoon soy sauce
3 cups sliced broccoli trunks and florets,
   cut into small pieces, blanched

In a small bowl, mix together the sauce ingredients. Set aside.

In a wok or large skillet heat the oil over high heat. When the oil begins to smoke, add the garlic and chicken. Stir-fry just until the chicken is cooked, 3 to 5 minutes. Add the noodles and soy sauce. Toss to mix. Add the broccoli and sauce. Toss to mix. Cook, stirring frequently, until the sauce is thick, 1 to 2 minutes.

Remove from the pan and serve.

4 SERVINGS

NOTE: Oyster sauce and fish sauce are available in most Asian food stores or from some mail-order catalogues.

APPROXIMATE NUTRITIONAL ANALYSIS PER SERVING

598 calories, 28g protein, 90g carbohydrates, 41g complex carbohydrates, 14g fat, 39mg cholesterol, 1942mg sodium, 791mg potassium

FILIPINO STIR-FRIED EGG NOODLES
(PANCIT CANTON)

Filipino cooking is a complex mixture of numerous Asian cuisines with just a touch of colonial Spanish influence. As in most Asian cuisines, noodles play an important role in the daily Filipino diet.

1 pound Chinese Egg Noodles (page 87),
   extruded through the angel-hair or thin
   spaghetti die, cooked al dente, drained,
   and rinsed under cold water

MARINADE

1 large egg white, lightly beaten
1 teaspoon soy sauce
1 teaspoon cornstarch

4 ounces boneless chicken breast, cut into
   $1/2$-inch cubes

SAUCE

$1^{1}/_{2}$ cups chicken broth
1 tablespoon fish sauce (see Note)

$1/8$ teaspoon freshly ground black pepper

3 tablespoons vegetable oil
4 ounces small raw shrimp, peeled and
   deveined
2 tablespoons finely minced garlic
1 tablespoon finely minced gingerroot
2 large scallions, green and white parts,
   cut into matchstick strips

4 ounces snow peas
1 large carrot, cut into matchstick strips
One 6-ounce can sliced bamboo shoots,
   drained and rinsed under cold water
$1/2$ teaspoon sesame oil

In a medium-sized bowl mix together the egg white, soy sauce, and cornstarch. Add the chicken and stir to cover. Let sit for 30 minutes. Drain and discard the marinade.

In a small bowl, mix together the sauce ingredients. Set aside.

In a wok or large skillet heat 1 tablespoon of the vegetable oil over high heat. When the oil begins to smoke, add the shrimp. Stir-fry until the shrimp turn pink, 1 to 2 minutes. Remove from the wok and place on a plate.

Add 1 tablespoon of oil to the wok. Add the chicken and stir-fry just until cooked, 3 to 5 minutes. Remove from the wok and put on a plate with the shrimp.

Add the remaining tablespoon of oil to the wok. When the oil begins to smoke, add the garlic, ginger, and scallions. Stirring constantly, cook for 30 seconds. Add the combined sauce ingredients. Bring to a boil and let cook for 5 minutes. Add the noodles, shrimp, chicken, snow peas, carrot, and bamboo shoots. Toss well to mix. Cook until most of the liquid has been absorbed.

Remove from the heat and place in a large serving platter. Drizzle with sesame oil.

4 SERVINGS

NOTE: Fish sauce is available in most Asian food stores and from some mail-order catalogues.

APPROXIMATE NUTRITIONAL ANALYSIS PER SERVING

620 calories, 32g protein, 80g carbohydrates, 70g complex carbohydrates, 18g fat, 208mg cholesterol, 1093mg sodium, 531mg potassium

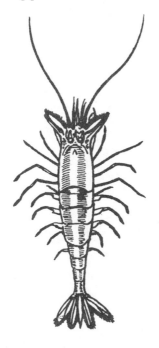

STIR-FRIED THAI RICE NOODLES
(PAD THAI)

Pad thai is without a doubt an excellent introduction to the rich and diversified cuisine of Thailand. This rice noodle dish, full of meat or chicken and shrimp, can be served as either a side dish or an entrée.

8 ounces Rice Noodles (page 89),
   extruded through the angel-hair or thin
   spaghetti die, cooked al dente, drained,
   and rinsed under cold water

SAUCE

1 teaspoon rice or white wine vinegar
3 tablespoons fish sauce (see Note)
1 tablespoon tomato paste

2 teaspoons sugar
$\frac{1}{4}$ teaspoon ground cayenne pepper

GARNISHES

3 tablespoons chopped toasted peanuts
2 scallions, white and green parts, thinly
   sliced

1 jalapeño pepper, seeded and thinly
   sliced
1 lemon, sliced into 4 wedges

Vegetable oil spray
2 large eggs, lightly beaten
2 tablespoons vegetable oil
1 tablespoon finely minced garlic

4 ounces coarsely chopped lean pork or
   chicken breast
4 ounces small raw shrimp, peeled,
   deveined, and coarsely chopped
1 cup bean sprouts

In a small bowl mix together the sauce ingredients. Set aside.

Prepare the garnishes and set aside in small individual serving bowls.

Spray a large 12-inch nonstick skillet with the vegetable oil spray and heat over medium heat. Pour in the beaten eggs. Cook until set. Remove from the pan and cut the omelette into 2-inch-long thin strips. Set aside.

In a wok or large skillet heat the vegetable oil over high heat. When the oil begins to smoke, add the garlic, pork or chicken, and the shrimp. Stir-fry until the meat and shrimp just appear done, 2 to 3 minutes. Push the mixture to the sides of the pan to form a well in the center. Pour in the sauce. When the sauce begins to bubble, stir to mix with the meat and shrimp mixture. Add the noodles and gently toss to mix. Stirring constantly, cook until the sauce is absorbed. Fold in the egg strips and bean sprouts.

Remove the pan from the heat. Serve with garnishes.

4 SERVINGS

NOTE: Fish sauce is available in most Asian food stores and from some mail-order catalogues.

APPROXIMATE NUTRITIONAL ANALYSIS PER SERVING

716 calories, 39g protein, 101g carbohydrates, 72g complex carbohydrates, 22g fat, 343mg cholesterol, 842mg sodium, 589mg potassium

DESSERTS AND BREADSTICKS

In my opinion, the best ending to a perfect meal is the perfect dessert. For a light yet sophisticated finale, try serving the raspberry crisp. For a more homey touch, noodle pudding will hit the spot. And for the holidays, do as the Neapolitans do and whip up a batch of *struffoli*, small pieces of fried dough covered with honey.

And for those with not much of a sweet tooth, perhaps some fresh fruit and cheese, served with crisp, homemade breadsticks made with dough from the pasta machine.

NOODLE PUDDING

Noodle pudding is one of many popular comfort-food desserts. Easy and quick to prepare, noodle pudding is also great for breakfast or as a snack.

1 pound hand-cut egg pasta noodles such as tagliatelle, maltagliati, or pappardelle, cut into 3-inch-long strips, cooked al dente, drained, and rinsed under cold water. (You can also use accumulated dough scraps left over from making shells for manicotti, cannelloni, and other egg pastas.)

⅓ cup golden raisins
5 large eggs
2 tablespoons unsalted butter, melted
½ cup sugar
2 cups milk
2 teaspoons vanilla extract

Preheat the oven to 350° F. Lightly butter a 10-by-8-by-2-inch baking dish. Layer the noodles in the dish and sprinkle with the raisins.

In a medium bowl whisk together the eggs, melted butter, and sugar until blended. Add the milk and vanilla extract and whisk together. Pour over the noodles and raisins. Cover the baking dish with foil and bake for 30 minutes, or until the custard is set.

Cut into squares and serve warm or at room temperature.

6 SERVINGS

APPROXIMATE NUTRITIONAL ANALYSIS PER SERVING

476 calories, 19g protein, 66g carbohydrates, 35g complex carbohydrates, 17g fat, 323mg cholesterol, 387mg sodium, 480mg potassium

RASPBERRY CRISP

The following recipe is an adaptation of one that I had read in *New York* magazine a few years ago. I found the use of won ton skins to be a novel, low-fat alternative to butter-rich pastry dough. Since won ton skins are so easy to work with, you'll find this dessert a breeze to prepare.

Although you will need only 12 crisps, the recipe allows for breakage and therefore calls for 6 extra won ton skins.

18 Won Ton Skins (page 85), 3 inches
   square

6 tablespoons unsalted butter, melted
½ cup sugar

FILLING

¾ cup low-fat raspberry yogurt
½ cup heavy cream, whipped stiff

SAUCE

6 ounces frozen raspberries, defrosted
1 teaspoon lemon juice
⅓ cup sugar

1 pint raspberries

Preheat the oven to 375° F. Line 2 large baking sheets with parchment paper. Cover with the won ton skins without overlapping. Brush lightly with the melted butter and sprinkle with half of the sugar. Turn the won tons over and repeat the process. Bake for 4 minutes in the middle rack of the oven. With a spatula, flip the won tons over and bake for 2 to 3 minutes, or until lightly golden. Do not let the won tons brown. Remove from the oven and cool on a wire rack.

Fold the yogurt into the whipped cream. Chill for at least 1 hour.

Put the defrosted raspberries in a fine-mesh strainer over a bowl. With the back of a mixing spoon press on the raspberries to force out the juice. In a small saucepan bring the juice to a boil and reduce by 50 percent. Add the lemon juice and sugar. Stir well to dissolve. Let cool to room temperature.

To prepare the raspberry crisps, pour a small pool of raspberry sauce around the perimeter of 4 cake plates. Place a crisp on the center of each plate. Put a rounded tablespoon of the yogurt–whipped cream mixture in the center of the crisp. Line the edges of the crisps with fresh raspberries. Place a crisp on top to form a sandwich. Repeat the previous steps to form another layer. Cover with a crisp. Garnish the top with a dollop of the yogurt–whipped cream mixture and 3 raspberries. Serve within 1 hour of preparation.

4 SERVINGS

APPROXIMATE NUTRITIONAL ANALYSIS PER SERVING

652 calories, 9g protein, 101g carbohydrates, 30g complex carbohydrates, 25g fat, 112mg cholesterol, 401mg sodium, 306mg potassium

FRIED NEAPOLITAN DOUGH BALLS
(STRUFFOLI)

Traditionally served during Christmas, *struffoli* are little balls of fried dough that are coated in hot honey, piled decoratively on a serving plate, and sprinkled with small colored sprinkles and candied citrus peel.

DRY INGREDIENTS

3 cups all-purpose flour
¼ teaspoon salt
½ cup sugar

LIQUID INGREDIENTS

3 large eggs, at room temperature
3 tablespoons vegetable oil

4 cups vegetable oil for frying

DECORATIONS

1½ cups honey
1 tablespoon colored confettini sprinkles
   (very small colored sprinkles)
1 tablespoon finely diced candied citrus
   peel

Following the instructions given in your owner's manual, prepare and set up the pasta machine with the breadstick extruder die.

Place the liquid ingredients in a glass measuring cup. If less than ¾ cup, add more oil to make up the balance.

All ingredients must be at room temperature. Add the dry ingredients to the pasta machine mixing bowl. Switch the pasta machine on. Slowly pour the liquid ingredients through the feed tube. Mix for approximately 3 minutes, or until the dough appears to be coming together in soft, pea-sized crumbs.

Following the instructions given in your owner's manual, begin to extrude the dough. Cut off the first 2 to 3 inches extruded and discard. As the dough begins to come out, gently move it away from the machine. Cut with a sharp paring knife or scissors at 8-inch lengths. Place the extruded dough in a single layer on a lightly floured work surface. Using a sharp paring knife, dipped periodically in flour, cut the dough into small, ½-inch pieces.

In a heavy-bottomed 2-quart saucepan heat the oil. Fry the struffoli in small batches in the hot oil. Turn with a slotted spoon to brown them evenly. Remove from the oil with the slotted spoon when evenly golden, and drain in a colander.

In a heavy-bottomed 2-quart saucepan heat the honey over low heat. When the honey begins to simmer, remove from the heat. Add the fried struffoli and stir to cover. Remove them from the pot with a slotted spoon and place decoratively in a pyramid or ring shape on a large serving plate. Sprinkle with colored confettini and candied citrus peel.

8 SERVINGS

APPROXIMATE NUTRITIONAL ANALYSIS PER SERVING

661 calories, 7g protein, 83g carbohydrates, 34g complex carbohydrates, 12g fat, 64g cholesterol, 89mg sodium, 91mg potassium

THIN BREADSTICKS
(GRISSINI)

As a bread baker, I have always appreciated freshly baked homemade breads. One of my favorite snack foods to make are breadsticks, especially the true Italian version, *grissini*.

Grissini are long, pencil-thin pieces of dough that are baked without having had a chance to rise. Because they are made with fast-rising yeast, grissini are quick and easy to make with the pasta machine, which kneads and shapes the dough.

DRY INGREDIENTS

1½ teaspoon fast-rise yeast, sifted with
3 cups bread flour
1 teaspoon salt

LIQUID INGREDIENTS

¾ cup plus 3 tablespoons water, blended with
¼ cup extra-virgin olive oil

Preheat the oven to 375° F. Lightly sprinkle two 13-by-9-by-1-inch baking pans with flour. Set aside.

Following the instructions given in your owner's manual, prepare and set up the pasta machine with the breadstick extruder die.

All ingredients must be at room temperature. Add the dry ingredients to the pasta machine mixing bowl. Switch the pasta machine on. Slowly pour the liquid ingredients through the feed tube. Mix for approximately 3 minutes, or until the dough begins to form small balls of dough.

Following the instructions given in your owner's manual, begin to extrude the dough. Cut off the first 2 to 3 inches extruded and discard. As the dough begins to come out, gently move it away from the machine. Cut with a sharp paring knife or scissors at 6-inch lengths. Place the extruded breadsticks in a single layer on a clean kitchen cloth and cover with another cloth.

Take a piece of the dough and place it on a lightly floured work surface. Starting in the center and working out to the ends, gently roll the dough back and forth with the palms of your hands, until it is smooth and approximately 12 to 13 inches long. Repeat until the dough is used up.

Place the grissini on the prepared baking pans in straight rows. Space ½ inch apart. Bake for 10 to 15 minutes, or until they are golden brown. Remove from the oven and cool on a wire rack.

ABOUT 36 BREADSTICKS

APPROXIMATE NUTRITIONAL ANALYSIS PER BREADSTICK

52 calories, 1g protein, 8g carbohydrates, 8g complex carbohydrates, 2g fat, 0mg cholesterol, 60mg sodium, 13mg potassium

The Guide to Perfect
Pasta, Noodles, and Dumplings

For best results, be sure to read and refer to the Introduction, especially Making Pasta Automatically (page 19), Taking It to the Next Step (page 22), Ingredients (page 24), and Tools of the Trade (page 26).

Problem:

Pasta machine labors while mixing.

Or Dough does not form small, soft, pea-sized shapes.

Or Pasta does not extrude or crumbles when extruding.

Reason:

Dough is too dry because:

1. Ingredient ratio is off, allowing for too much dry ingredients and not enough liquids. The approximate ratio of dry to liquid is 4 to 1. This means ¼ cup liquid should be used to every cup flour.
2. Ingredients were not properly measured.
3. Extruder die was not soaked in hot water before making pasta.

Solution:

1. Continue mixing. Add additional water, a teaspoon at a time, until the dough appears to have a smoother consistency.
2. Refer to the Introduction (pages 25–26), on how to measure dry and liquid ingredients properly, then follow Solution 1 for immediate remedy.
3. Always soak the extruder die in a small bowl of hot water for a few minutes before making pasta. This helps the dough come out smoothly.

Problem:

Dough is sticky and it is coming together in one large ball.

Or The extruding pasta sticks together.

Or It is very sticky to the touch and not smooth when extruded.

Or Pasta (especially lasagne and linguine) has jagged edges.

Reason:

1. Ingredient ratio is off, allowing for too much liquid ingredients and not enough flour. The approximate ratio of liquid to dry is 1 to 4. This means that only ¼ cup liquid should be used to every 1 cup flour.

2. Flour has a high moisture content.
3. Potatoes, when making gnocchi, are too moist.
4. Dough is too sticky.

SOLUTION:
1. Stop extruding and add an additional 1 to 2 tablespoons of flour. Knead for a couple of minutes before extruding. If still too moist, add a tablespoon or two of additional flour.
2. If problem is ongoing, change brand or source of flour. If you live in a high-humidity area, gradually increase the amount of flour called for in the recipes until you find a suitable dry-to-liquid ratio. Modify the recipes to fit your needs.
3. Only use baked russet or Idaho potatoes. Weigh the potatoes before cooking them (this can be done in the store when being purchased) or use a kitchen scale. Do not overknead, since this can cause the dough to become too soft. See Solution 1 for remedy. Do not add too much flour, though, since gnocchi will become too heavy.

PROBLEM:
Flavored pasta ingredients are not evenly mixed throughout the dough.

REASON:
They were not evenly distributed when added to the other ingredients.

SOLUTION:
1. When adding finely minced herbs or cooked, chopped spinach, sprinkle evenly over the dry ingredients in the pasta machine mixing bowl before beginning to mix.
2. Vegetable purées, pesto, and tomato paste should be well beaten with the other liquid ingredients after they have been measured.

PROBLEM:
Some extruded pastas like penne, ziti, and lasagne curl when extruded.

REASON:
This is the way some models extrude the dough.

SOLUTION:
1. Gently try to bend the pasta to make it straight as it is extruding.
2. Grab the lasagne between your index and middle fingers while it is extruding. Gently pull it away from the pasta machine, keeping it straight while doing so.

PROBLEM:

After having extruded well, pasta stops coming out.

REASON:

When extruding through some dies with small openings, the dough can take a longer time to extrude and can overmix, becoming too soft and forming large balls or clumps. This makes it difficult for the dough to fit through the extruder.

SOLUTION:

Stop the pasta machine. Open the lid and tear the dough into small, marble-sized pieces and drop them toward the front of the mixing bowl near the extruder opening. You may have to do this a couple of times to extrude all of the dough.

PROBLEM:

Hand-cut pasta does not stretch when rolled out by hand.

REASON:

1. Extruded dough is too dry.
2. Gluten needs to rest.

SOLUTION:

1. Always make sure that the dough is smooth and elastic. If it is not, add additional water. Extruded pasta should always be covered with a clean kitchen cloth until you are ready to roll it out. This way it will not dry out and/or become brittle.
2. Never try to hand-roll pasta dough immediately after extruding. Let the dough rest for a few minutes to relax the gluten so that the dough will stretch effortlessly.

PROBLEM:

Extruded pasta breaks up when cooked.

REASON:

Dough was too dry.

SOLUTION:

The next time you make pasta, follow the recipe more carefully. Measure the ingredients properly to assure the proper ratio of 4 parts dry ingredients to 1 part liquid.

PROBLEM:

Pasta sticks together and/or tastes soft and gummy after being cooked.

REASON:

Pasta was cooked too long.

SOLUTION:

Only cook pasta until it is al dente, which means it should be somewhat chewy. Cooking times vary depending on the thickness of the pasta. Test for doneness every couple of minutes while cooking.

PROBLEM:

Stuffed pastas like ravioli and won tons split open when cooked.

REASON:

1. They were not properly prepared and sealed.
2. They were not properly stored or cooked.

SOLUTION:

1. Do not overstuff with filling. Always seal well by squeezing the edges tightly. If edges do not stick together, wet lightly with water.
2. Do not stack more than two high when storing. Place a piece of waxed paper or parchment between the layers. If they are frozen, do not defrost them before cooking. Carefully drop them into a pot of lightly salted, boiling water.

SOURCE DIRECTORY

ALTHOUGH ALMOST ALL OF THE INGREDIENTS YOU will ever need to make wonderful homemade pasta, noodles, and dumplings are available at your local supermarket, you may need to seek out a couple of special ingredients.

If you live in or near a large city, seek out its ethnic neighborhoods to find such ingredients as dried Italian porcini mushrooms, Asian fish sauce, or rice flour. Health-food stores and food co-ops are also sometimes a good source for less commonplace grains and flours.

The following mail-order companies are also useful sources of hard-to-find flours like durum wheat and other pasta-related ingredients. I have also included a couple of excellent sources that offer Italian and Asian ingredients and foods.

The Great Valley Mills
RD 3, County Line Road
Box 1111
Barto, PA 19504
(800) 688-6455

Established in 1710 as a grist mill, the Great Valley Mills offers a catalogue with a wide variety of high-quality, family-grown-and-produced foods and grains from Lancaster County, Pennsylvania. They are an excellent source of quality pasta flours like durum wheat and semolina. They also prepare and sell flavored pasta mixes.

King Arthur Flour Baker's Catalogue
Sands, Taylor & Wood Company
Box 876
Norwich, VT 05055
(800) 827-6836

King Arthur is the ultimate baker's ingredients and accessories catalogue. It offers a near-endless variety of flours, herbs, spices, and accessories. Most ingredients can also be used in making pasta, especially flours like buckwheat and semolina. Even if you do not buy anything, it's great just knowing they are out there!

Dean & DeLuca, Inc.
560 Broadway
New York, NY 10012
(800) 221-7714

Purveyor of some of the best-quality foods in New York, Dean & DeLuca also has a mail-order catalogue that offers a wide selection of foods, such as porcini mushrooms, sun-dried tomatoes, meats, and cheeses, and kitchen accessories and gadgets that can be used in making and preparing pasta.

Zabar's
2245 Broadway
New York, NY 10024
(212) 496-1234

Zabar's, New York's famous kitchen emporium, well known for its vast offering of appliances, cookware, gadgets, and food products, sells some of its offerings by mail-order catalogue.

The Oriental Pantry
423 Great Road
Acton, MA 01720
(800) 828-0368

While most supermarkets carry soy sauce and gingerroot, other Asian ingredients may be more difficult to find. Look no further: the Oriental Pantry offers an extensive selection of hard-to-find Asian foods and sauces.

INDEX